RENATA MOLHO
Translated by Antony Shugaar

Being Armani
A Biography

Baldini Castoldi Dalai
Publishers since 1897
www.bcdeditions.com

Text © 2007 Baldini Castoldi Dalai *editore* S.p.A. - Milano

All rights reserved. Reproduction of the whole or
any part of the contents without written permission
from the publisher is prohibited.

All attempts have been made to contact copyright holders
of photographs included in this volume. Credits that have
been obtained appear in their respective captions.
In future printings the Publisher will gladly credit
copyright holders not identified herewith—
please contact the Publisher directly
with missing information.

ISBN 88-978-6073-296-5
Library of Congress Cataloging-in-Publication
Information is available from the
Library of Congress upon request.

Printed and bound in Italy by
Grafica Veneta S.p.A. - Trebaseleghe (PD)

To Bouby, Adriana and Rudolf

Contents

CHAPTER 1	**Origins**	11
CHAPTER 2	**A Decisive Meeting**	33
CHAPTER 3	**The Adventure Begins**	53
CHAPTER 4	**Discovering America**	77
CHAPTER 5	**Dark Years**	103
CHAPTER 6	**Another Identity**	121
CHAPTER 7	**Staying Faithful**	145
CHAPTER 8	**Conquering the World**	175
CHAPTER 9	**Thinking of the Future**	211
	Bibliography	235

CHAPTER ONE

Origins

Giorgio Armani conquered the world of fashion. But though in time he would devote his life to his work and become the subject of talk and gossip, his vocation was the result of a series of decisions that were dictated by necessity and, more often, chance.

Giorgio Armani was born sixteen months after the death of an infant sister, Silvana. The time was 7:20 on the morning of July 11, 1934. The Armani family lived on the Via Colombo in Piacenza, in the area renowned for the statue of the Fascist she-wolf. That year marked a high-water mark for Benito Mussolini's dictatorship. The next, Italy invaded Ethiopia, setting the stage for Italy's alliance with Nazi Germany in the Second World War.

A Cancer with Leo rising (there was a new moon at his birth), Giorgio shared his sun sign with his two siblings—his older brother, Sergio, and his younger sister, Rosanna—born on June 29, 1929, and June 27, 1939, respectively. He had much to say about their relationship: how close they were and yet how independent. The age differences meant that they had different sets of friends, though they also enjoyed moments of great happiness together. Though guided by a great respect for individuality and personal space, they still cultivated and preserved unshakable bonds with each other.

Their father, Ugo Armani (who died in 1962), was a civil servant who worked for the Fascist Federation. He and his brother had played soccer for two local teams, the Edera (Ivy) team and later the Piacenza team. Giorgio's mother, Maria Raimondi, was a housewife every bit as athletic as her husband and active in social causes. She helped to run the local summer camps for city children, taking in the occasional stray. "She would give them a scrubbing and clean them up, because they were clearly children of families without money," Rosanna, very young at the time, recalled.

Both parents loved the theater. In fact, they first met onstage, performing for an amateur theater company in Piacenza. The theater was a recurring topic of family conversation. Giorgio's paternal grandfather, Lodovico (oddly enough, Giorgio's maternal grandfather, a furniture maker, bore the same first name) manufactured nineteenth-century-style wigs for the city theater. He enjoyed taking the children behind the scenes with him, and it was inevitable that Giorgio would fall under the spell of the theater's atmosphere and color. "I remember going to the Piacenza theater, a venerable old municipal theater, similar to La Scala, though smaller. I couldn't have been older than seven or eight, and I liked to spend time there. I loved the smell of the stage."

Significantly, Armani also remembered his horror at the ugliness of the wigs his grandfather created, their contrived and unabashed falseness. This precocious manifestation of aesthetic sensibility foreshadows the artistic process he would later adopt when he set about inventing his style. His fabled adherence to reality, to the way people really live, so much a part of his fashion, is perhaps a product precisely of his abhorrence of falsehood and artifice. In fact, Giorgio Armani worked by subtracting, removing, refining. He even stated at one point that his chief sources of inspiration were the things he disliked, because it was in the effort to improve that he found his sense of equilibrium. But this was the stuff of the hidden future. Childhood was not the time for such niceties. "We focused on a few basics: getting enough food to eat, finding inexpensive school textbooks, and finding a way to go to the movies on Sunday. We couldn't afford much."

The movies were an important source of diversion during Armani's early years. When he was little, they opened up a world into which he loved to escape, but they were also a source of instruction, and their lessons are at the crux of his existential and professional makeup. "I still remember how excited we were as children," Armani recalls, "when the announcement was made in the early morning: perhaps, this afternoon, we're going to the movies."

The first movie he remembers seeing is *The Iron Crown*, by Alessandro Blasetti, "a sort of pacifist fantasy" named best film at the 1941 Venice Film Festival. "It was magnificent, everything was staged at Cinecittà, including the 'valley of the lions,' and the great actor Gino Cervi played the cruel tyrant Sedemondo. I was overwhelmed by the richness of the lighting, the sheer incredible splendor of the scenes, and of course all those beautiful women: Elisa Cegani and Luisa Ferida. I was eight years old, and it made such a deep impression that I had dreams about it."

Among the films he remembers is the German movie *The Adventures of Baron Munchausen*, his first movie in full color. "I only managed to see half of it. It was the end of the war, and we had been evacuated to a small town called San Nicolò, about twenty miles outside of Piacenza. One Sunday we managed to make it to the movies, and this is what was showing. I loved it, but suddenly the air raid siren went off, and it was goodbye movie. We all ran as fast as we could for the shelters."

After the war, American movies started to appear. Armani, eleven years old, discovered cowboys—who left him cold, as did musicals. "I didn't care for Italian neorealism either; it was drab and depressing. All it offered was the same reality of ruins and rubble that I already experienced on a daily basis. It was not until much later that I understood the importance, and the innovative power, of these films, so different from everything being shown on the silver screen at the time." Even so, Vittorio De Sica's *The Bicycle Thief* captured his imagination: "When that little boy, played by Enzo Stajola, asks his father for ice cream, or when he squeezes his hand in the middle of the crowd that presses in on him after he steals the bicycle, it just breaks my heart."

Piacenza, given its strategic location, was one of the main targets for Allied air raids during the Second World War. The first bombs landed on the Piazza Duomo (the cathedral square), Via Chiapponi, Via XX Settembre, Via S. Antonino, and Via Sopramuro: Piacenza's historic center was devastated. A subsequent air raid destroyed the train station, the bridges over the river Po, and the town arsenal. The years passed, the war raged, and Piacenza was hit by a total of ninety-one raids. In all, 1,214 Allied planes dropped bombs on the city, 206 people were killed, and hundreds of homes were destroyed.

"The war changed everything. It was hard, very hard," Armani recalls. "I witnessed the deaths of two of my friends in a bombing raid. With my sister, Rosanna, three years old at the time, I experienced a strafing run. We were in the street; an airplane flew over us. We threw ourselves into a ditch. I was little and I protected my littler sister. It was traumatic. Bombs were constantly falling down on us." Another memory: "Once we were riding our bicycles in the street when some planes flying at low altitude spotted us. I got off my bicycle and I put my sweater, made of green terry cloth, over my head. If I can't see them, then they can't see me, is what I thought to myself." His early memories are permeated with a sense of continual emergency, running and fighting for his life: "At three in the morning, all of us children who lived in the building found ourselves together, with our blankets, down in the bomb shelter. Once we got over the shock of being so rudely awakened, though, it was sort of fun."

Giorgio's mother, though strict when it came to raising and educating her children, transformed the dire events that marked their everyday wartime reality into enjoyable adventures, a kind of improvised game. Rosanna recalls: "She managed things as if she were putting together a picnic for her three children. When the air raid siren sounded, I was supposed to get the dog, Giorgio was supposed to get me, Sergio helped to carry all the things we needed, and then we all just bolted for the air raid shelter."

Sergio, the oldest of the three Armani children, had a lively, strong personality, and he assumed the role of leader. Tall and sturdy, reckless and daring, with curly hair, he looked like Joseph Cotten and may have been his mother's favorite. Giorgio was a little shy, with straight hair and his maternal grandmother's light blue eyes. He was slighter than his brother and more reserved at school, though there are stories of how he made use of his crushes on his female schoolteachers in elementary and high school, winning their affection to the point where it helped his grades. Once, when he was walking by his old high school in Piacenza, the Liceo Ottorino Respighi, Armani is said to have told a friend about his old Italian literature teacher: "She had a wonderful face, with a sweet, open expression; she wore her hair gathered in a great crown of braids, the way they used to in the nineteenth century. I was so in love with her, I would dream about her, and she wasn't completely indifferent to me, I have to say. I was a lazy boy, and every Monday, instead of turning in my homework, I would come up with the most ridiculous excuses. And she would answer, smiling sadly: 'It's all right, never mind.' "

Giorgio gives Sergio credit for initiating him into the mysteries of theater and film: "My brother would organize little stage shows, he loved the movies and the theater, and so he would draw us into his creative efforts." Together, they would build little villages with lead toy soldiers, inventing characters and designing houses. They also constructed a little puppet theater of rags and pieces of wood where they would put on shows in Bolognese dialect. The leading actor was always a certain Fasolein (*fagiolino*, or "little bean," in dialect). In all this, Rosanna was at best allowed to be a spectator, if she wasn't simply chased rudely out of the room by Sergio or dismissed more kindly by Giorgio, "who always had a gentler nature," as she recalled. There was a subtle rivalry between the two boys, but they were always closely allied against their sister—at least until Sergio grew older and more independent, leaving his younger siblings to spend more time playing together.

Sergio was especially gifted as an actor, and he would provide the voices for dozens of characters; Giorgio's talent was for making and manipulating the figures. The brothers staged the shows in a canonry made available to them by Don Pietro, their parish priest; sometimes they even had a live audience, who gained entry with tickets for admission handmade by Sergio and Giorgio. As Rosanna remembers the shows, "they were never battles, they were stories of a little village, and each character had a name—this one was the baker, that one was the priest. They described slices of ordinary life, and the conclusion was always a bombing raid." In wartime as in peace, children's games are based on the events that surround them.

Armani had always been skillful with his hands. In an interview she gave in 1982 to an Italian newsweekly, his mother recalled an early morning surprise. One day, as she was making the beds, she noticed that the bedcovers were missing some of their fringe. Giorgio had cut it off to make hair for his puppets. "As a little boy, he would play with erector sets, with a drill, with toy soldiers, but he especially liked to use his hands to make things. He knew how to make all sorts of things. He would go to the Mercato di Senigallia [a well-known Milanese flea market] and he would come home with some old broken-down thing. Two days later, we were all amazed to see how he had transformed it. In the evenings, I would go to bed and I could still hear him hammering, pounding: in the morning, his bedroom looked like hell, but he had built himself a sort of loft."

Among the many episodes of his childhood in Piacenza, one from Giorgio's eleventh year was especially memorable. This is how his sister recalls it:

> Once, when the all-clear had sounded, and the air raid alarm was over, my mother asked Giorgio to take me home. She was going to go by a friend's house to get something, I can't remember what. We crossed the street, and in the Corso Garibaldi, where we lived at the time, there was this little, very narrow lane. At the

corner was a movie house, where they were showing *Snow White and the Seven Dwarfs:* I stopped to look at the movie posters and a friend came over to call my brother. I wanted to go with him down that little alley, but an older girlfriend held my hand, reassuring me: "No, Rosanna, wait. Giorgio is only going around the corner." But then, as soon as he had vanished from view, maybe three minutes later, there was an insane, terrifying roar, all the windows were shattered, and the scorched, black silhouette of my brother emerged out of the smoke. One person died. What had happened was that a group of boys were playing at blowing things up, little things they made with gunpowder; they would go off like firecrackers. But the friend who had called Giorgio had leaned over to get a better look, and the packet with the gunpowder had dropped right into the fire. It was inevitable that a huge explosion followed. That boy died, another boy was wounded by flying glass, and my brother was badly hurt. Miraculously, he survived: he was in the hospital for forty days, they thought he was going to lose his sight. I still remember all the evenings and days that we spent in the hospital. I was five years old. I even remember picking up one of his sandals, because only one had stayed on his foot. My mother asked me: "Where is Giorgio?" and I answered "He's in there, and this is his sandal." The therapy was horrible; they used alcohol. I always heard him screaming, it was just awful, they would practically immerse him in alcohol, and then pick off the burnt flesh. At that age, it was almost fun to be in a hospital. There were nurses who would give me toys. But I remember that my mother was in a pitiable state. And my brother was swollen up, his head was just huge! It was weird.

When he was finally released from the hospital, Giorgio could only walk with crutches—which hooligans stole, because his father had worked for the Fascist Party. "I dragged myself home, leaning on the walls and weeping at the pain," Giorgio recalled.

This literally searing experience left Armani with a scar on one foot and a slight sensitivity to strong light. No doubt it marked him emotionally as well. Indeed, Giorgio's early life was at times starkly dramatic. In a recent interview, he thought back to his first love. "She was a little girl with the body of a boy, an olive complexion, and huge, exotic eyes. She was nine years old, and I was twelve. She was adorable, and I remember I was already designing the furniture for our future home. One day, she was riding her bicycle and she failed to notice that the truck that was overtaking her was pulling a trailer. She veered back out onto the street as it passed, and she was crushed. I can still see her pretty face in my mind's eye."

Perhaps as a result of all this intense experience, Giorgio was a boy who liked to listen rather than express his views openly. He was an observer, timid, introverted, and keenly aware of everything going on around him. He was also restless, never contented, always looking for something, whether a rare checkered shirt or a special texture in his relationships with others. These qualities are still integral to his personality after all these years. They are fundamental to his complex character: he is immensely adaptable, yet he seems incapable of real satisfaction with what he achieves. He always thinks there must be something more.

When Giorgio was eleven, his father, Ugo, a very private man, was sent to prison for eight months, as punishment for his role in Fascist politics. Giorgio recalls:

> I still have that steel fence before my eyes, and my father behind it, clustered with the other inmates. I remember the tears that streamed down his face, his helplessness, his shame. We would go to visit him on Sundays, but we could hardly ever understand a word he said. In the babel of voices, it often happened that one prisoner would answer a question that was meant for another prisoner. Then we would walk back home in silence, hugging the walls, as if we had committed some terrible crime. Those were scars that marked the whole family. Deep scars. I can still feel, physically, the confusion that overwhelmed me. I was eleven years old, what did I know about politics? It seemed unfair that Poppa was in prison. But it also seemed unfair that we children should be mixed up in it. It was a tragedy, and it was a tragedy that was bigger than any of us. In fact, I can still remember the sense of unease, the guilty feeling, the tremendous embarrassment that I felt one time when we were all walking home from the prison. My brother and I knew that they were showing a movie at the theater that we wanted to see. Walking home with our mother, we were terribly sad; we had even seen our father weeping, holding both her hands in his, through the bars. But then, there was that movie that we both wanted to see. I would have given anything to go to the movies. Right away. Immediately. Perhaps it was a reaction to the moments of terrible sadness that I had just experienced.

I wanted to escape, and I knew that a movie would help me to escape. I was walking along next to my brother, my head hanging down, looking sidelong at him, and hoping that he would be the one to mention it to my mother. But we couldn't do it. We were afraid to tell her how badly we wanted to go to the movies. In fact, we felt as if it was sacrilegious even to mention it.

In a 2002 interview, an Italian journalist asked Armani whether his family was Fascist. He explained that back then nearly everyone was Fascist and that he thought his father might have paid a higher price for being a Fascist than many others did. He added that the huge Fascist assemblies gave not only the adults a sense of belonging but the children as well. "In that period, everyone felt that they had an important role to play in the destiny of the nation. Later, much went wrong, but the feeling persisted. Even today, I find nothing not to like in the Italy of those years. In the Italy of today, on the other hand, I see no good faith and no admirable feelings in the politics."

After the grim period of imprisonment, Ugo Armani moved to Milan, where he had managed to find work as an accountant for a shipping company. Perhaps it was during this period that Giorgio's mother became the central figure in the family. Ugo's absence during the week was painful, but Maria managed to make her children's lives pleasant even during the hardest times. In that dark climate, when "things were black or white; there was a left and a right," her focus and strength were crucial: "She never let us feel as if we were underprivileged just because there wasn't much money. She always made us feel comfortable. She was a wonderful mother, not oppressive. If it's possible, with her silence she taught us a great deal, more than if she had talked and talked. She was a very beautiful woman, but she devoted herself heart and soul to her family, to us children. This was a very important lesson for me."

Demanding, not given to coddling, she inspired her son both personally and professionally. Dressing her children in clothing made of old parachutes and military uniforms, "she made us sports shirts and shorts with a khaki fabric that at the time was called 'coloniale,' and we looked every bit as good as our wealthy friends. Perhaps my love of sober, discreet, understated clothing came, subconsciously, out of that childhood memory—out of my mother's ability to send us off to school, well dressed, though with what little she could afford, since we were a poor family." His own early fascination with uniforms also played a part in the fashions he created so many years later: "Whatever the case, I felt quite elegant in the uniform of the 'figlio della lupa,' or sons of the she-wolf; it had a sort of rigid white bandolier and a large 'M' in black lacquer. I didn't like the uniform of the 'balilla,' which was too drab and anonymous."

Giorgio Armani's proverbial sense of proportion may derive from his mother's talent for making the most of everything, for making even the simplest thing something special. "I remember a family outing, perhaps the only one we ever took. We drove out in a wonderful automobile, all leather and shiny metal, probably the property of one of my father's friends. It was an old car from the thirties. We had parked the car on the lakeshore, and we were eating frittata. I have a fantastic memory of the magnificent sky, the light blue of the lake, the smell of frittata and leather upholstery." His childhood memories are studded with references to the everyday life this solid, unswerving woman organized for him.

Giorgio attended the Liceo Ottorino Respighi, and he often took care of Rosanna, who was going to a religious school run by Ursuline nuns. The unshakable bond that still links brother and sister dates to the unforgettable times they spent together back then: long bicycle rides, excursions from Piacenza to Rivergaro (where Andrea Camerana, Rosanna's son and the current marketing and licensing director of Armani, later married). Days spent together building huts out of branches, playing in the sand, or playing rugby on the banks of the river Trebbia became precious memories for the children, who even now still express their sense of gratitude for the serene stability their mother worked so hard to conjure for them. The river Po ("A horrible place," Rosanna says ironically, "I only saw the sea when I was much older"), with its tranquil landscapes, was the background to this childhood idyll, even when the war forced evacuation to the countryside around Piacenza. And its quiet waters were the setting for an experience that Giorgio still remembers tenderly: "There, on that island, at the age of seven, while swimming in the river, I watched my first love scene."

At the end of the forties, the family was finally reunited in Milan.

> We began a new life. It was a city where people lived separately, the rich all together, the middle class all together, and the poor all together. It was a tough time for our family. My parents were struggling to rebuild a decent life after the war. Milan seemed like a big, tough city, very different from the peaceful life in our small town. This is where I grew up, professionally and physically. The part of Milan that I lived in was the "città di ringhiera," an older section known as the "zona

Ticinese," where my father worked. Then there was a sharp division between the center of the city and the outlying quarters. You would see third-run movies out there. The center was for a small elite. There was no flow of people to the center on a Saturday afternoon; people stayed in their own neighborhoods. That type of city stayed with me.

The world of Giorgio's adolescence bore little resemblance to today's. He spent Sundays with his friends, enjoying the city parks and experimenting with photography. They never left their neighborhood: "We didn't live in the wealthy part of Milan; in fact, we lived in the poor part of town. It was a small quarter, where you had your own friends. A place to play soccer, a local movie house, where you went to the movies because you didn't have enough money to go to the center of Milan. There were friends' houses where you showed up with a bottle of whiskey, a record player. That was how we had our first romantic experiences, when our parents were out of the house." Everything was fresh, everything was new. "I wore my brother's hand-me-downs. We didn't have enough money to buy things. I understood how my parents were struggling, and I was worried about our problems, our difficulties." None of this made him self-conscious, though; the social differences that distinguished him from some of his schoolmates were never the cause of envy or suffering.

Giorgio attended the science high school—the Liceo Scientifico Leonardo da Vinci—where he enrolled in 1949 in Class 2A. A classmate, Aldo Battecca, remembers that he was a good draftsman. "He was a boy who was easily distracted and, while the teacher taught the lesson, he would fill page after page with drawings." Pietro Ponti, who sat next to him, remembers his love for photography. Already pronouncing his "r" in the French style, Giorgio did well in French class, but he flunked math, physics, and science. All his fellow students, though, remembered him as a likable guy, lively and open. They also remembered that he didn't like sports, except for tennis. And he never missed a soccer match among friends.

Though tested by crises successfully overcome, tempered by the challenges of life, and raised in a climate of sober serenity, Giorgio had no clear idea what he would do when he grew up. He was slightly confused—not very self-aware, as he would later say himself—attractive but without passion for anything. His aesthetic sense, however, was already keen. He still talks about his endless dissatisfaction with the way his mother—who herself had great instinctive style—set the table; he always had his own opinion of how it should be done. And even though fashion was still far in the future, it is clear that Armani already looked at the world through an aesthetic lens, demonstrating a modest but marked inclination for what would become his future. Well dressed and groomed, very elegant, his friends remember that he always wore an impeccable gray vicuña suit. Giorgio Bratina—who enrolled in medical school with Armani and later became a pathologist—recalled how Giorgio stood out from the other students. "He certainly had an inborn elegance, and this made him different from us. He already wore trousers without cuffs, and a T-shirt with a horizontal cut, while we wore the standard clothing that our parents bought for us. He had his own tailor; we bought ready-made clothing from the department store. He was always amazed at my cuffed trousers, and thought they were completely outmoded. One day he managed to persuade my mother to send me to see his tailor, who made me a fashionable suit, under Giorgio's supervision, with a bird's-eye pattern. I never had anything like it again in my life."

Giorgio was very popular with the girls, but he never fell in love. He found it easier to be friends with them, giving them invaluable advice on how to dress and do their hair. "His first girlfriend was a little blonde, with a proper well-to-do air, and she was always perfectly groomed, too," recalls Rachele Enriquez, a journalist and close friend of his. "She had a pleated skirt, and whenever she sat down or stood up, it was wrinkled. It would drive Giorgio crazy: a rumpled skirt! He already had this need for perfection." Anna Maria Vendola, another classmate and one of Giorgio's confidantes, reported that "he really enjoyed styling his mother's clothing—she was a beautiful woman—and later [did] the same for his baby sister. What he did wasn't that major, but he would make little suggestions, and sure enough, he was always right." Would it be premature to see in these comments the first evidence of the great fashion designer to come?

It was the 1950s, and Giorgio's life was simple. In the season when the narcissus bloomed, he and a group of friends would go up to the mountains over Como to spend the afternoon gathering flowers. No one owned a car, so everyone took trains or buses. In the winter, sometimes people would go skiing, getting to the slopes however they could. They had to get up at four in the morning, then take a city bus to get to the long-distance bus for Bardonecchia. There were no big facilities, and for every improvised descent on old wooden skis they had to walk back up the mountain for the next, since ski lifts were lacking as well. These excursions were rare, however, and people were more likely to stay in town. Often they would gather at the Armani house. "He lived in the biggest apartment back then, in the Via Druso," Rachele Enriquez remembers.

"Rosanna had pigtails, shorts, and that turned-up nose that the Armanis all have; she would turn it up even further, and walk by, paying no attention to us," says Enriquez. This petite and lovely little girl soon became a renowned model—for years, the cover girl of the weekly magazine *Arianna*—and she could have been a movie star. She is said to have turned down a major studio contract that Alberto Lattuada offered to her; she preferred her freedom and limited her roles to a small part that fell in her lap in the movie *Rocco and His Brothers* (Luchino Visconti, 1960) and another "with her name on the movie poster" in Eriprando Visconti's movie *Una storia Milanese* (1962).

"Sergio, the older brother, was completely out of our league," Enriquez recalls. "He was tall and just fascinating. There were no televisions in the houses; we exchanged ideas and books. One friend was crazy about classical music, and he would show up with a stack of seventy-eight rpm records, with Beethoven's Sixth Symphony, directed by Toscanini, and we could just sit in religious silence listening to it. Or else we'd push the sofas back, pull up the carpets, and dance." Social interaction was encouraged by the lack of the distractions we take for granted now. Giorgio enjoyed taking pictures of his female friends, seeing to their makeup, styling them, wrapping them in his mother's white ermine stole. You can smile at the naïveté of those portraits, but now they appear highly significant. Those were the years when Giorgio bought his first Lambretta, a joint purchase with Sergio: "We thought it was the coolest thing. When I would drive it around town, I felt such a sense of freedom. ...I never dreamed I would become someone, conquer anything. I had just turned twenty and, as was natural, my sole ambition was to earn a few lire so that I could put some gas in the tank of my Lambretta."

"There wasn't a lot of leeway at the time. If you were a man, you needed to become a notary, a lawyer, or a doctor," Giorgio recalled. Sergio was studying law, and, influenced chiefly by the hero of A. J. Cronin's novel *The Citadel*, Giorgio decided to become a physician. He had a romantic idea of the profession, imagining himself as a country doctor, working to protect the weak. Even as a little boy, he had shown a curious interest in anatomy. One of his favorite games was to make little doll figures out of bits of dried pasta; inside them he would hide a coffee bean. "That coffee bean represented the illness, which I would have to find and treat." Giorgio enrolled in the Department of Medicine at the University of Milan, but he broke off his studies in his third year ("I found a huge obstacle in my path: the anatomy exam"). While waiting to figure out which direction his life would go, he decided to join the army.

He left home with a romantic idea of barracks life as well. In his head, he had scenes from the movie *From Here to Eternity* (Fred Zinnemann, 1953): "I even brought my tennis racket with me. But it wasn't much like the movie." He joined the Corps of Combat Engineers as a private and was stationed first in Siena and later in Riva del Garda. Thanks to his medical studies, he was promoted and transferred to the regiment's infirmary in Verona. At first, "it seemed that military life there was just boredom, and not the romantic idea of comradeship that I had imagined, the idea of great men weeping hot tears. I was almost always alone in the infirmary, and I spent most of my time painting. Then a flu epidemic broke out, and suddenly there were seventy patients to take care of." Giorgio Armani found himself injecting soldier after soldier as one after another of his comrades were admitted to the infirmary. This experience with hospital life, contrasted with the occasional enjoyable evening at Verona's famous Arena, convinced him that medicine was not the career for him. "Medicine was not the best field of study for Giorgio," his mother recalled. "He persisted with his usual stubbornness, but he seemed sad, he wasn't the same. So we urged him to stop studying medicine, and I couldn't sleep for three nights running: Were we doing the right thing by telling him to forget about it? If only God would give some guidance. My husband kept telling me: 'Children have to do what they want, you can't meddle, otherwise you'll do more harm than good.' And in fact, if we had advised Giorgio to stay the course, to become a doctor, we would have been wrong. Even though I think he would have done well in that field too."

He was handsome, and he loved the movies. Perhaps he could have become an actor or a director. With a hint of regret, he later said: "Becoming an actor was an impossible dream. The situation wasn't right, and it was another world, far from the expectations of a middle-class family, and not an especially prosperous one." A responsible and conscientious son who had great respect for his family, for the silent and dignified way it faced problems, Giorgio needed to figure out how to fend for himself. "I didn't want to think that my mother and father were sacrificing anything because of me." All he wanted was an opportunity to make a little money. His glorious future was not only distant but totally unimagined: "In my beginnings, there was no fire in the belly for fashion. I really didn't want to do fashion at all."

CHAPTER TWO

A Decisive Meeting

Why fashion, then? Apparently, fate insisted. Giorgio was still serving his obligatory term in the Italian military when, determined to find a job during a short leave, he confided his frustration to his longtime friend Rachele Enriquez. He had shared many youthful adventures with Rachele, who had served as an amateur model for him during his early, somewhat awkward forays into photography.

Rachele worked at La Rinascente, a major Italian department store, and she knew they were looking for help in the advertising office. Giorgio was not about to miss this opportunity. He talked Rosanna into posing for a few photographs and then brought them along to the interview he had managed to secure. "I believe in fate," Giorgio Armani stated many years later. "The photographs were awful, but the person who was in charge of advertising at La Rinascente was very powerful, and he liked me. He knew that I was no photographer, and that Rosanna was not a model at the time, but he helped me to land the job." Thus happenstance and enterprise combined to launch a career that knows no equal: in 1957 Armani started work at La Rinascente, where he remained until 1963. "I happened to wind up working for a department store," Armani would later say, crediting pure chance with the way things turned out; after all, at the time, any open door that offered him a possibility of economic independence he would have been likely to stride through without a second thought.

He was soon made assistant to the architects who worked for the Milan department store. One of these was Giancarlo Ortelli, with whom Giorgio discovered many traits in common, among them, a degree of reserve and tastes that ran to the rigorous, the sober, and the spare. Many years later, Giorgio asked Ortelli to renovate the former Palazzo Riva, in the Via Borgonuovo, where he moved his residence and offices in 1982.

Stubborn, determined, and dependable, Giorgio managed to complete his military service and still hold on to his job. He found he had much to learn:

> When I started work at La Rinascente, I believed that everyone was good-hearted, that when someone smiled at you, they were really smiling deep down. Then I learned that this wasn't true, that sometimes people smiled at you because they were supposed to smile; but just because they were smiling didn't mean they cared, and sometimes that smile might hide something much worse. It was truly a university of life, teaching both good things and bad. I also learned how to get along with other people: I had grown up in a very private, intimate, protective family environment, and suddenly I found myself surrounded by old and hardened buyers, and truly ferocious women....Perhaps in part because of my innocent air, I always managed to win others over. And it is safe to say that that was the beginning of my career.

Giorgio Armani's arrival at La Rinascente coincided with its rebirth. It was the early sixties, and the Italian department store was evolving into more than a sales outlet. Once an influential institution, it had run out of steam, and a great change was under way. "Until that time, for the people of Milan the store had been a place to go to buy underwear and undershirts, identical bolts of cloth, men's suits that looked like uniforms." La Rinascente began to cater to the sophisticated taste of Milan's *alta borghesia*, or upper middle class, a style that till then had been restricted to a privileged elite, found only in the drawing rooms of the well-to-do. Taking their cue from its American and Swiss counterparts, Micio Borletti and Cesare Brustio, owner and managing director, respectively, reimagined their store. It became an entry to a larger world, the combined creation of architects, industrial designers, advertising talent, managers, and researchers (among the top names working for La Rinascente were Roberto Sambonet and Giancarlo Iliprandi). La Rinascente was responsible for the birth of the Golden Compass, today still a respected award for the finest designers.

It was a piece of luck that Giorgio happened along precisely when things were beginning to change. Although at first he was relegated to the perimeter, just one more new hire, Armani fell in love with the sense of the new and found encouragement in that intellectually stimulating environment. "Choosing a fabric, judging a combination, encountering new styles—this was a time of major shows within the department store—were all exciting new things. I understood it, and I was good at it." In later years people would minimize his contribution when asked what he did at La Rinascente, their recollections perhaps tainted by the resentment so often reserved for the successful. Giorgio Armani, they would say, designed window displays. "That isn't true, he did much more than that," Franco Savorelli recalls with passion. Savorelli met Armani in 1959 and went on to work with him for many years. "He came to La Rinascente to work in this world [of fashion] and he was responsible for shaping the image of the department store. He reported to the architect Giancarlo Ortelli, who was in charge of Rinascente Immagine; Giorgio became something like an assistant to this group of creatives, which was also in charge of the display windows."

Armani worked in a variety of capacities, ranging from junior photographer to overseeing the preparation of the window displays and purchasing for the men's clothing department. "At first I worked as an assistant to the window dressers. Then I supervised their work. Soon after that, I was moved over to the fashion department, where I worked as an assistant to the buyers. My job was to help them maintain continuity in their purchases and to create an appropriate atmosphere for the fashion designers themselves." Finally, in the so-called Fashion-Style office he was put in charge specifically of men's apparel. "Starting from a position of complete ignorance, I made my way on my own, and I can tell you it wasn't easy. I knew nothing about designing, except for the ornamentation that I had done at school, and I had been very good at that. I never attended art school, I never apprenticed in the ateliers. I learned everything on my own, and it took time."

As his world became larger, Giorgio was forced to refine his notions about lifestyle, clothing, society, and even dreams and ambitions. He had to learn to anticipate what people needed and what they wanted. He began to study the mechanisms of fashion and manufacturing, the rules of production and distribution. One of Armani's most influential colleagues was Gianni Bordoli, the marketing director of La Rinascente. Bordoli was responsible for many of the innovations at the store. He grasped, among other things, the importance of having designers and buyers work side by side to improve the quality of the store's offerings. A very elegant individual, Bordoli exuded a whiff of eccentricity that appealed to the young Armani's imagination. With an air of nonchalance, he would wear soft, unconstructed jackets, "rather similar to the jackets I made in later years," Armani admits.

Armani's thirst for beauty and his demanding standards of harmony, already so evident in his personal life, began to find expression on a larger stage. In this public dimension that opened onto the broader world, Armani was selecting the finest products from the United States, India, and Japan—countries still relatively unknown to the Italian buying public—and adding them to the array of La Rinascente's offerings. Making his first trips outside of Italy—to France and Spain—he was especially impressed by Avignon and Gaudí's Sagrada Familia, in Barcelona. Among his first and most noteworthy gambles was the decision to import those yellow vests—worn with tweed jackets—that had previously been unique to London, the benchmark of style for the younger generation. This first success gave him the confidence to continue.

His gift for observation proved very useful: "I noticed that there were some really good designers working in France. I had no experience. I wasn't working with major fashion figures, with a fashion staff: I was working with artisans. I was terribly afraid of getting it wrong. After my period of time at La Rinascente, word got around that I was good at what I did." Perceptive and open-minded, he soon learned to pay close attention to the relationship between quality and price, and he was always on the lookout for new ideas. Inventing new ways of displaying and exhibiting his finds, all the imagination he had once devoted to the home theatrical productions he once staged with his brother now found an official purpose, a growing audience, and open recognition.

Giorgio Armani has always had a special bent for elegance, whatever form it might take. His aesthetic has also had a significant influence on the company he has kept. He likes remarkable women, and among those he recalls with gratitude and pleasure is Adriana Botti, "who is still modern today, mysterious, charming, dynamic, sunny, and intelligent," as Rosanna Armani describes her. "She looked like Silvana Mangano. She was the head of the public relations office under Gianni Bordoli; she played basketball in CUS Milano, with me. She had done a screen test for Antonioni, but he finally chose Lucia Bosè. Giorgio was a little bit in love with her." It was Adriana who introduced Giorgio to Nino Cerruti, a textile manufacturer who was looking for an assistant to work on Hitman, a new line of men's clothing he was starting up for his family company.

Cerruti was an ambitious young industrialist working in men's and women's fashion who already—in the midsixties—had a Paris address, on the Rue Royale: his was the first Italian company to have a presence in Paris. The Cerruti name was prestigious, a concern with a great corporate tradition, an impressive catalog of achievement, and a carefully groomed image. With Hitman—offices in Corsico, near Milan—Cerruti was the first to conceive of a tailored men's ready-to-wear line in an otherwise barren men's fashion landscape. At the time, the only men's clothing available for import consisted of rigid, standardized, unexceptional ready-to-wear; the single alternative, for those who could afford it, was to have one's wardrobe custom-made by a tailor.

"You strike me as a smart young man," Cerruti said to Armani at the interview. "You'll do well." Then he picked up the fabric samples that were lying on his worktable and asked Armani which one he liked best. "Luckily," Armani remembers, "I picked the fabric that he liked too. And so I got the job." Cerruti is an intuitive and farsighted man, but he is also reserved and modest: whenever someone says he was responsible for discovering Giorgio Armani, he says it isn't true, all the credit should go to the special talent of that young man who, whatever happened, would inevitably have gained renown. "He had a natural talent, he was self-taught. He would have made a name for himself in any case. Men like Armani are so rare that when one emerges, even a blind man notices."

And so Giorgio began to design men's clothing for Hitman, after a one-month training period in the factory. He worked for Cerruti for eight years, until 1970, "selecting lighter and lighter fabrics, in cooler and cooler colors, discarding internal structures, moving buttons, whittling down shoulder pads, giving the men's jacket—till then, a formal, rigid, almost embalmed piece of clothing—a loose and comfortable appearance, youthful, designed for all ages," as Lucia Mari later wrote. It was a foundational experience for Armani, ideal training for the revolution that he would soon unleash. "As I perused the fashion magazines, I realized that there was a gulf between what the public wanted and what the magazines were showing. This was a time when I was beginning to develop clear ideas and opinions about fashion. And the world of fashion was beginning to notice my work. I worked in complete freedom and independence for the Hitman collection. It brought in a lot of money, and there was quite a sizable turnover." Though only a few of the items designed by Giorgio Armani made their appearance on the

French runways—Cerruti was one of the first Italians to hold runway presentations in Paris—the fashion journalists encouraged him, saying they could pick out his designs among the clothing in the other collections they had seen.

In the seventies, an advertising campaign for Hitman began a new chapter in fashion communications, even though it was misunderstood at first. "The campaign used photography by Oliviero Toscani. It featured a close-up of a long-haired man. You can see the hair moving slightly, but not his face. The headline read 'Hitman by Giorgio Armani.' It was a straightforward image, and immensely successful. At first, though, everyone said to me, 'Armani, you're using a photograph that doesn't show the clothing. No shoes, no fabrics. We make fabrics, we make clothing!' I still have that photograph. For the public, it was a radically new approach. It took courage for Toscani to do it. Nowadays, you can see lots of fashion advertising like this, but at the time it was really innovative." The idiom, the lexicon that eventually conquered the world, did not yet exist. Even the Italian word for fashion designer—*stilista*—remained to be invented. Nino Cerruti was one of the first to use the word, giving it an entirely new connotation. He would introduce Giorgio Armani as "my *stilista*." And this was an unprecedented development. "This was a line of work that no one had ever heard of," Armani recalled. "And to tell your relatives, or your friends, or even your mother 'I'm going to be a *stilista*' was something totally mysterious, unknown. You couldn't convince them that it was a good career. I held out, though, and I have to say that the way things turned out proved me right."

Giorgio was growing, both professionally and personally. No longer the insecure young man of the early days at La Rinascente, he bought himself a secondhand Porsche convertible and let his hair grow long (it was still chestnut brown then, though it would turn white when he was still young). He would go to the office late, a signal of his growing sense of freedom. Everywhere he went, his dog—a boxer—went with him. Disciplined and meticulous, he learned to distinguish among fabrics and how to work with them. He became skilled at identifying their potential and making the best possible use of them. He began to design clothing that lent itself to mass production. Working alongside Nino Cerruti—who trusted him unreservedly—he came to understand just how important it was for a young fashion designer to have a company working with him, supporting him and producing his work.

Fashion journalist Natalia Aspesi wrote about Armani's early years, "His career was methodical, not spectacular. It moved gradually, in the shadows. It was the solid career of a hardworking employee, inventing, day by day, a new profession, in the years of Italy's economic boom, a time of individual miracles, the dawn of the corporate and financial fortunes of fashion." And that career remained unassuming until Giorgio began to stand out from the crowd. Even at this early juncture, it was possible to glimpse his rigorous aesthetic, and the lessons of designing menswear for Hitman served him well. He soon started to work with other brands, and the most magical and surprising runway presentations of the early seventies at the Sala Bianca in the Pitti Palace in Florence were those held by the various manufacturers—Montedoro, Sicons, and others—for whom he was designing collections. Even if his name was not yet officially attached to the work he did, everyone knew the applause was for Giorgio.

Already Armani was conceiving a softer, looser fashion, keyed to the spirit of modernity yet inspired by the style of his mother. A number of close friends recalled that he had a special fondness for a particular snapshot of his mother holding him in her arms as a baby. The image of woman, slightly masculine, captured in that photograph had always attracted him. His fashion reinvented the look he found there, a revised retro spirit that removed all the rigidity and excesses of construction typical of the time, imagining a softer form. It was the beginning of the seventies, and Armani presented his leather jacket, treating the leather as if it were fabric, completely revolutionizing how this material was used in clothing. Deconstruction was on its way.

The stage was far less crowded than it is today, and it took only a few talented young people to invent a new world, impart a different rhythm to things. The decade between 1960 and 1970 contained within it the seeds of all that is still with us. Two images encapsulate the entire story: the moon landing (1969) and the final scene in *Zabriskie Point,* Antonioni's 1970 film. The former represents the great leap upward, the technological, physical dream, the joy of garnering new knowledge, and the widespread diffusion of news affecting the planet at large. The latter, in which the most emblematic consumer goods are launched skyward in a historic explosion, put everything into question, discarding traditional values and proposing new ones of a moral and political nature. Until that point, the world had seemed sufficient, relatively orderly, perhaps suffering a few tremors in the wake of rock and roll but in general still pastel, still rigidly defined, with rich people dressing as rich people and poor people dressing as poor people. Everything was strictly identifiable, separated, with distinct social divisions: the categories were neatly arranged, by exclusion or by invitation. Fashion was one of the great discriminating factors. Haute couture spoke to only a few, but it was the dream of the masses. Those who lacked the money and resources to follow high fashion tried to imitate it, ignored it, or dressed modestly; the aesthetic canons were indulgent, and fashion was influenced more by barely attained necessities than by the whims of a narrow elite. Fashion was experiencing one of the most ambiguous moments of its existence, torn between its chief purpose—distinguishing the elites—and the new desire to dress the largest possible number of people. This led to the industrialization of fashion that the French would call *prêt-à-porter* (derived from the American term *ready-to-wear*), and very few would immediately understand its significance.

André Courrèges showed a collection in February 1965 that was constructed "for the future," for women of the "cosmic" age. Like Courrèges and Paco Rabanne, Pierre Cardin, too, placed great faith in new materials—such as plastic, vinyl, and metal—and experimented with new technologies (among other things, Cardin designed the early clothing of the Beatles, the jackets with the Korean collars). In 1968 he launched the surprising Cardine, a preformed suit, cast in a mold, without stitching, adorned with permanent impressions. He prophesied "the end of cutting and stitching." Cardin said: "For me, the expression *haute couture* has sounded as false to me as *harpsichord* or *horse and carriage*. The changes in lines, the disguises, the rise and fall of hemlines—that's all just so much camouflage. The true creation is the evolution of technology, the true creator is someone whose discoveries can be immediately industrialized." One of the leitmotifs of avant-garde fashion of the sixties is precisely this faith in technological progress and the power of industry to solve the problems linked to the expansion of consumption.

New conceptions of the boutique also came into being around this time, among them Laura, opened by Sonia Rykiel, and Dorothée Bis, founded by Elie and Jacqueline Jacobson.

The press was seized with enthusiasm for the developing scene, and it shoved haute couture aside, relegating it to a minor role. At one end of the Kings Road, in Chelsea's Sloane Square, is the Royal Court Theatre, where John Osborne's *Look Back in Anger* had inaugurated in 1956 a new genre of theater that focused on the lives of the English working class. Hanging out around the theater was London's beatnik tribe, haunting a recently opened array of Kings Road pubs. Ernestina Carter of the *Times* of London described them as follows: "Long-haired, bearded young men wearing leather pants and leather jackets, with even longer hair, young women wear short tight skirts and black tights or high black boots, under skimpy, shabby little overcoats."

Mary Quant decided that this was the mood and the sensation she wanted to express. Her store Bazaar, also on the Kings Road, dated back to 1955. She invented a new style of fashion that satisfied consumers' wishes at a relatively low price, showing that what mattered for a consistent look was not just clothing but also makeup, hairstyle, and an appropriate attitude. Soon her signature logo, the daisy, became the symbol of an era, along with the spiky short haircuts of Vidal Sassoon. The miniskirt, developed at the turn of the sixties, took on a great emblematic significance. And fashion, which till then had been the privileged domain of the French, suddenly became a British monopoly. "We were at the dawn of a huge movement toward rebirth in the field of fashion. It wasn't anything that we were doing," Mary Quant later said. "We just happened to be part of it."

Numerous cheap boutiques opened in London. One was Biba, opened in 1964 by Barbara Hulanicki. There were also other, more expensive boutiques, such as Quorum, run by two former students from the Royal College of Arts, Ossie Clark and Alice Pollock, the stomping ground of the richer members of the pop scene. Launched by the mods, Carnaby Street in Soho established itself as the street for alternative fashion, with clothing inspired by such pop stars as the Beatles, the Who, and the Rolling Stones. In Italy, everything arrived later, translated and domesticated by Elio Fiorucci, who opened a shop in Piazza San Babila in 1967, right in the heart of the most conservative and respectable neighborhood in Milan.

In all this, designers focused increasingly on how to mass-produce clothing, how to make it convenient for daily life. Fashion was increasingly becoming a mass-market phenomenon. Designers talked more and more about numbers, consumption, and mass production. Everything was boiling over, intermingling, including movies and fashion. In 1964 Francis Wyndham interviewed the three fashion photographers David Bailey, Terence Donovan, and Brian Duffy for an article in the *Sunday Times*, "The Model Makers." An extended version of Wyndham's tape recordings was the research source for Michelangelo Antonioni's *Blow-Up*. David Bailey, who had been identified in *Vogue* in 1963 as a "new-wave photographer," told Wyndham that his own work had been inspired by movies like François Truffaut's *Jules and Jim* and Fellini's *8 1/2*. And the fashion editor Marit Allen, while still in school, had seen Jean Luc Godard's *Breathless* and been totally captivated by it. The emblematic film of the nouvelle vague had a "major influence" on her. The pacing of Godard's movie was transported into fashion photo shoots. "Spontaneity and fluidity" were precisely the qualities that Allen sought in fashion. The informal and agile imagery captured by the handheld movie camera in *Breathless* led to the adoption by many fashion photographers of the 35mm reflex camera.

Photographers took their models out into the street, capturing them for posterity in the midst of traffic and other real-life settings while preserving unchanged the essential artificiality of the shoot. While, on the one hand, everyone was dreaming about Anita Ekberg in Federico Fellini's *La Dolce Vita* and a social life punctuated by parties and the opulent, rich decadence made immortal by *8 1/2*, on the other, the female figure became spare and sticklike, increasingly childish or androgynous. Just seven years after the publication of Vladimir Nabokov's novel, *Lolita* became familiar from Stanley Kubrick's 1962 film version.

In the sixties, a decade that is still quoted today and is widely considered a source of continuing inspiration, there were only two certainties: everything was possible, and dissatisfaction was intolerable. A revolutionizing discourse on roles, geography, and time was transforming the perception of the world. An unprecedented wave was rolling out from university campuses, a new form of nomadic thought sweeping across continents and countries, no longer the domain of institutional politics or single personalities. Fashion was seriously endangered: it represented consumer culture and middle-class aesthetics. Important political and historic events were taking place, and fashion was branded as frivolous and cynical. Balenciaga, at the peak of his career, closed down his atelier for a full twelve months in 1968, the year of the student revolt in Paris. Old uniforms and vintage clothing suddenly appeared in used clothing stores, ennobled by time and wear. In conservative Italy, which always seemed a bit behind, Armani managed to synthesize all this turbulence, tame it, strip it of all subversive aspects, and restore hope and trust in an aesthetic that followed the winds of change using a style that was authoritative but flexible, in keeping with the spirit of the time.

The press of the time was as vital as the world around it, and experimentation was aimed at genuine discovery. In 1967 in Italy Flavio Lucchini, one of the few authentic talents in fashion publishing, founded *L'Uomo Vogue*. A thoroughly innovative magazine, there had never been anything like it. The memoirs of Gisella Borioli, who joined Condé Nast as a proofreader, graduated to editor, and finally became editor in chief, describing a meeting with Armani at the beginning of his career, offer a sense of what it meant to work in fashion at the time—a time when the horizon was vast and uncluttered, when creativity was the only important resource. The year was 1968:

> I met Armani when he was still an assistant to Cerruti at Hitman with Pinotto Marelli [the marketing director]. He was in charge of fabrics and manufacturing. As the assistant of Flavio [Lucchini], I would go to the offices of Hitman, and there, while the bosses talked to one another, I would be assigned to Giorgio Armani, who was the assistant. We were equals, and together we would go to select the items and outfits to publish. He would show them to me, very polite, very shy, but even then, confident, precise, and very smart. At the time, we were making up fashion as we went along at *L'Uomo Vogue:* we would identify the aspects in women's fashion that seemed right to carry over to men's fashion. Often, there was nothing that worked and we would find someone to help us develop it, from Procopio—who was already making ties with the faces of Mao, or Coca Cola, it was the time of Pop Art—to Guarnera, who would make

shirts with Lichtenstein silkscreens. And Hitman would sometimes develop themes just for a fashion layout. Armani would work with me to develop these ideas. Pinotto Marelli trusted him implicitly. We had established a relationship of great respect and friendship."

Always diffident, Giorgio describes the Armani of that time as someone who dressed "normally," "according to my resources, with a few touches of elegance, occasionally verging on the ridiculous, perhaps older than my age; I was still just a kid. Those were the years of tailoring, of the British style."

The seven years with Cerruti were crucial to Giorgio's development and education, but the pivotal moment of his professional and personal life was about to arrive. "The truly wonderful thing was to make it on my own. It wasn't easy to leave my safe job, which, though it wasn't all that complicated, paid very well. I had no experience in design or business. But I was young and naive, and that made it possible to look for new opportunities. I had no idea of the risks I was running, and my lack of experience prepared me psychologically for a change. I realized that as long as I stayed with Cerruti, I had relatively few chances of increasing my creativity. And then I met Sergio Galeotti." This was the crucial event of his life.

Sergio Galeotti was Tuscan, a great talker, so extroverted that he seemed the exact opposite of Giorgio: where the one was slight and impulsive, determined and positive, with a face that regularly broke into laughter, the other was compact and chilly, elegant but reserved, cautious and wary of expressions of feeling. Galeotti was born in Pietrasanta, near Lucca, and studied at the art high school in Carrara; he arrived in Milan in 1967. He started as a draftsman in a prestigious Milanese architectural studio, Banfi, Belgioioso, Peressuti, and Rogers, but soon changed professions completely: first taking a job with Pier Giorgio Mora, who imported fabrics from Scotland and India, and later working for the Larus chain of stores owned by Larus Miani. "I was a buyer, and I was earning more," Galeotti explained.

About ten years younger than Armani, he sparkled with an enthusiasm that was contagious. No one who met him failed to respond to his overwhelming exuberance, his generous nature, his infectious optimism, and his love of life. And Giorgio was no less enchanted. Captivated by Galeotti's charm, he shared with him a long portion of his life, both personal and professional. Lightning struck in 1966 at the Capannina in Forte dei Marmi; their partnership only ended with Sergio's death in 1985.

"Galeotti was a very sexy man," says Cristina Brigidini, a close friend of Armani's and editor in chief of *L'Uomo Vogue* in the years of his most spectacular success. "He had a very pure love for Giorgio, almost the love of a son." Irresistible and overwhelming, Galeotti managed to persuade Giorgio Armani to leave Cerruti. "I heard from everyone that he was really talented; and so I told him that the time had come to take advantage of the fact," Galeotti recalled. "He was already earning a lot of money, but he was hesitant about starting a business of his own. It took me a whole year, but I finally managed to persuade him." By this point, Armani was aware of the limitations inherent in his current position, half full-time job, half freelance career. Moreover, he had matured, he had learned, and he knew the time had come to strike out on his own. And so, encouraged by Sergio Galeotti and guided by his own daring, at the turn of the seventies Armani left his job with Cerruti to open a small office with Sergio in the Corso Venezia, where he served as a freelance consultant for a number of fashion manufacturers— Allegri, Bagutta, Gibo, Hilton, Montedoro, Sicons, Spirito, Ungaro, Ermenegildo Zegna, and Loewe, a Spanish manufacturer— while continuing to design for Hitman, all the while creating his own line.

Many, it seemed, would have preferred to keep Armani tucked away, a profitable secret, a designer of invariably successful collections for others. Among the eyewitnesses to Giorgio's entrepreneurial debut was Count Franco Savorelli, who remembers meeting Galeotti and Armani on the Via Lazio in Milan, where they lived. They asked him whether he thought an independent fashion line had a chance of success. As unquestioning as his faith might have been in the talent of Giorgio Armani, Savorelli couldn't entirely support the undertaking, pointing out the element of risk in any new venture. "But you are at the peak of success!" he said. Sergio, eager to venture into the unknown, replied drily: "Which is why he should do it!"

In 1969 and 1970 the Basile label was the top name in Italy. Muriel Grateau was the designer, taking her inspiration from Saint Laurent. Basile was the name to conjure with, comparable, say, to Tom Ford in the nineties. Gigi Monti, the strategist for Basile, understood the importance of expanding runway presentations to include a broader audience and the foreign press, but the Pitti Palace was too small and at the time Florence had no more suitable venues. Together with the already much-copied Missonis, Basile decided to move to Milan, a city flourishing in the new climate of change. In two or three years, Florence was on the decline—not to return to life for many years—and a new fashion era was dawning. This was the moment Giorgio Armani chose to take his place on the stage.

CHAPTER THREE

The Adventure Begins

Giorgio Armani finally went into business with Sergio Galeotti in 1975: July 24 saw the founding of Giorgio Armani S.p.A. Saturn was in conjunction with both sun and moon, casting a benevolent influence on the undertaking, as both astrologists and sales figures would later confirm.

Launching their adventure with scanty financial means, Giorgio and Sergio found themselves obliged to sell Giorgio's Volkswagen Bug to pay for the new business, setting up offices in the Corso Venezia, at number 37, in a tiny space they had rented for 1.5 million lire per year. "We sold everything we could get rid of in order to buy a worktable and a few lamps to furnish the studio, which consisted of two rooms, one of which was a business office for Sergio, and the other room, the design space, where I did my job. But I could hear him talking to the buyers, and he could hear me swearing when I couldn't get something right at the drawing table. It was a family operation, but it was wonderful." What they couldn't buy, they jury-rigged. A legendary story has Giorgio adding spots to a solid-colored fabric when the first collection demanded polka dots but they lacked money to get the real thing.

In this tiny office space, the team consisted of Armani, Sergio Galeotti, and Irene Pantone, who worked as secretary, administrator, and even in a pinch runway model. Irene still works for the Giorgio Armani company. Now, she is the corporate memory, but at the time she was a student, and Galeotti remembered: "We could afford to pay her so little because she was allowed to study while she was on the job."

Roles were defined from the beginning: Sergio was the manager, Giorgio was the artist. But everyone knew that already—or did they? Many years later, in an interview for *Vanity Fair*, Armani admitted that Galeotti had no experience whatsoever in marketing and sales. "Of course, I was there behind him. But to the eyes of the world—for him as well—we encouraged the idea that Sergio was the big sales guy in charge of the company. And I was the creative guy." As it happened, Sergio Galeotti proved very skillful in managing the marketing and sales division of the company, leaving Armani totally free to focus on his work: "He gave me the time to design, and he would manage customer contacts. He couldn't speak a word of English. And he had complete faith in what we were doing. I remember that he refused to sell one of my first collections to a major department store. We were nobodys, unknowns, but he told them that they hadn't reached the minimum order. I could hear him explaining it in the background, and I wondered to myself: What is he doing? What is he saying? This is the biggest department store, and he's telling them no!" From the very beginning, Galeotti set the rules of the game, with great confidence. In the process, he was completely overturning the old way of doing things.

Of course, Armani's glorious career would have been impossible without his creative genius, but the debt his success owes to his extraordinary relationship with Galeotti should not be underestimated. "From the very beginning, he made me feel like a father. And I immediately felt that I was responsible for him, that I needed to take care of him," Armani said, speaking about his first meeting with Galeotti. "It was as if he were my son." Sergio had left his family and the city where he was born, he had abandoned his career to entrust his fate to Armani: "I was responsible for this young man and for his future. I didn't want to betray his trust. That is why Sergio came to Milan to work with me. And, unexpectedly, our relation became one of profound affection." But that wasn't all. "It is a complicated blend of personal and professional elements, devotion and material success," as Judy Bachrach wrote in *Vanity Fair*. "An astonishing affinity," Armani adds, continuing, "The term *love* is too narrow. We were allies, in the face of life and the rest of the world."

They met and they fell in love. Countless anecdotes depict the tenderness, the kindness, the delicacy of the bond that united them: "Once we were walking down the street, and it was very cold out," recalls Cristina Brigidini. "Giorgio was wearing a light jacket, and Galeotti had on an overcoat. He took off his coat and put it on Giorgio's shoulders: 'Here, Giorgio, you'll get cold.' " To those who knew them, it was clear that Sergio Galeotti and Giorgio Armani were so different that they fit together perfectly. They shared everything, even their love for the small Sicilian island of Pantelleria, where they went on holiday in 1975 and decided to buy a small house, the first of the magnificent assembly of *dammusi*, the traditional structures of Pantelleria, where even now Armani spends most of his summer holidays, surrounded by friends and colleagues.

Theirs was already a solid partnership when they founded the company. "They lived in the Via Santa Cecilia, behind the Via Borgogna (it was only later that Giorgio went to live in the Via Borgonuovo, in the palazzo that once belonged to Felicino

Riva), and one evening they invited us to come over to dinner to show us their new apartment," Gisella Borioli recalls. "They were clearly two men living together; each one had a bedroom of his own, his own bathroom, and there was a big kitchen. They got along very nicely, very naturally; it was a pleasure to be around them. Sergio had little love affairs on the side, but Giorgio was faithful and rigorous about the relationship. Male couples, however, weren't such an open thing at the time, and they never made a big deal about it." Barbara Vitti, who worked with Armani for many years, remembers: "Even after their romantic relationship ended, no one ever heard Sergio say a bad thing about Giorgio or vice versa. Their friendship was more important than anything else; they argued and fought, of course, the way all partners do, the way everyone on earth does, but there was clearly a truly remarkable mutual respect. The intensity of their relation changed form over the course of time, but it remained substantially intact." They came to be like two brothers. Each one had love affairs, but this did nothing to disrupt their bond.

"They were two completely different personalities: Sergio was so lovable and funny," Vitti recalls with warmth. "He was always ready for anything.... Say he called me up one day, and I suggested to him, 'Let's run an advertising campaign in *L'Unità!*' [a Communist daily] he would reply 'Of course!'— and we ran the campaign. He just treated every new discovery with such enthusiasm. With Sergio, you just became best friends and then he was close to you. Giorgio, on the other hand, had a more restrained personality; he was a little more arid. It was as if showing his feelings cost him some effort. Not Sergio, he was right there all the time." Vitti continued, "I remember once that a woman friend of mine, a fashion journalist, was involved in a very serious car crash. He didn't even know her, but he sent me a note in an envelope with a few million lire—thousands of dollars, and this was years ago—and the note said: 'At times like this, perhaps, the most useful thing is money. Take the money to her, but don't say it comes from me.' He was incredibly generous, he was always open with everyone: if someone had a problem, at work as well, they would go to see Sergio. That's not to say anything bad about Giorgio," she concluded, "that's just his personality!"

But in what context was all this taking place? The seventies were difficult years for Italy, especially for Milan, a city that, as it attempted to become a fashion capital, was at the same time—as Natalia Aspesi recalls—"the epicenter of the most tragic social and political struggles and strife." From 1969 until 1975, Italy suffered 4,384 acts of political violence against persons or property. About 85 percent of these acts of violence took place in just six of Italy's ninety-four provinces and especially in the cities of Milan, Turin, and Rome. Of the events that occurred in these years, 83 percent were openly claimed as the work of neofascist extremists, backed by political powers; during that same period the neofascists committed sixty-three political murders, out of a total of ninety-two in Italy overall. Nearly all the massacres took place in that same six-year period (with the exception of the bombing of the train station in Bologna in August 1980) and produced 42 percent of the victims of terrorism. In 1978, in Rome, Aldo Moro, the head of the Christian Democratic Party, was kidnapped by the Red Brigades. All his bodyguards were murdered; later, his body would be found abandoned in the trunk of a car.

At the same time, problems in the Italian and world economy were becoming increasingly worrisome. In part, these stemmed from the cascading energy crisis triggered by OPEC, whose oil-producing member nations had decided for the first time to test their power to hurt the industrialized nations of the West. In part, as always, the travails afflicting the economy were a result of the structural conflicts inherent in the Italian system, which struggled in the early seventies with shortages of investment funds, high rates of inflation, and problems with the balance of payments.

Fashion was of no interest to anyone at the time, and it was completely overlooked in the press and the mass media. "Such fragile commercial figures as fashion designers seemed anachronistic, out of place," as Natalia Aspesi wrote, looking back. When they put on ready-to-wear, the matrons of the middle classes favored designs in the French style of Yves Saint Laurent; Italian fashion was a poor relation. Middle-class ladies, Aspesi adds,

> still ruefully aware of the rotten eggs that demonstrators splattered on their glittering evening gowns at the historic season-opening performance at La Scala in 1968, tended to disguise themselves when they went out on the street, wearing anonymous, unremarkable clothing. Young women who were dreaming of freedom through feminism and other political movements had tossed out their respectable pleated skirts and their cardigans, and now wore only stiff afghan jackets, badly matched with tie-dye dresses from India. On behalf of the revolutionary cause, they were willing to forgo being attractive: all of them, that is, except for a very young Miuccia Prada, who would hand out leaflets for the Italian Communist Party dressed in French haute couture. Prada was very

courageous to do that, because young, well-dressed women were considered to be Fascists at the time; they became pariahs, and were occasionally treated to insults and actual physical attacks.

Outside the offices overlooking the Corso Venezia, the street scene was turbulent and even frightening. Inside, Armani, leaning over his worktable, worked intently with pencils and swatches of sample fabrics to give shape to his first ideas, making do with the limited resources at his disposal. Turning his back on the world around him, he was developing what would in time become his unmistakable style, as distinct from the fashions of the day as it was removed from the din of shouted slogans and the wafting clouds of tear gas that filled the streets of the city. Perhaps he heard snatches of the sounds of the student protest movement, reports of occupied university campuses, of factory workers and labor unions battling the industrialists, but he maintained his intense focus.

In July 1975 he presented his first menswear collection, for spring-summer 1976, in a tiny showroom on the Corso Venezia. And the miracle took place. "That first season, lots and lots of people came. There were a few *vestieriste*, or assistants, but basically it was just us—Sergio, Giorgio, Irene, and me—and we took care of everything," remembers Count Franco Savorelli, who worked alongside Armani and Galeotti in the first skin-of-the-teeth years. But although the collection was an instant hit among reviewers, as Galeotti remembered later, "it practically took every last cent that we had. We sold virtually nothing."

Gisella Borioli remembers how, in that first runway presentation, Armani handled women's clothing:

On the runway, there were women and men together; it was a really small presentation. For the men he had made soft, loose trousers and jackets. The collection was already a beautiful thing to behold. It looked different. Maybe that was a product of his time with Cerruti, the use of the materials, the deconstructed look...it all worked very well. The female models, on the other hand, were wearing little matronly outfits, sort of typical of the Milanese bourgeoisie, sort of something by Walter Albini in a minor tone. But the following season, the womenswear looked more modern too: in the first official presentation, the womenswear was already moving 180 degrees in the opposite direction: slightly masculine style to the clothing, with deconstructed blazers, designed for a woman executive, a woman with a career.

That first womenswear presentation, also for spring-summer 1976, was held three months later in an old Milanese restaurant in the Piazza del Duomo, the Ristorante Carminati. "There was a significant detail in that first collection," Anna Piaggi later recalled, "even if it was ever so subtle, and slightly ironic." This collection featured the first jackets for women, and in the same runway presentation a number of male models wore terry-cloth suits in garish colors. It was a crossbreeding of genders: the feminine touch softened the men's fashion, while a hint of masculinity added force to the designs for women. Armani did it with a light touch, subtly introducing subversive ideas that slithered into the subconscious, transforming the collective imagination on a physiological level. In March 1976 the autumn-winter runway presentation, in the halls of the Hotel Palace in Milan, introduced tweed women's suits. The jacket had a decidedly mannish cut, but it was lightened and softened by the pleated skirt. This is how Armani remembers that moment: "Maybe it was no big thing, but at the end of the presentation, Galeotti put on a record that he picked at random, which was very popular at the time: by the Inti-Illimani. The twelve female models all walked out onto the runway together, and started moving to the bouncy beat of the music. To our amazement, we heard a burst of applause."

Taking inspiration from the highly personal and nonconformist style of his sister, Rosanna, whom he greatly admired, and looking ahead to the future role of women in a rapidly changing society, Giorgio invented a different kind of women's jacket that won immediate success. It was a translation of the men's jacket: using traditional masculine fabrics and constructed with the same flowing line, though the proportions were changed, it conferred an unprecedented authority on the female figure. Armani had another memory of that debut: "We had the feeling the public was willing to accept an Armani label. I hadn't just jumped into the void, coming up with ideas off the cuff. I set out with some very clear ideas about what I wanted to see women wearing. It seemed to me that they had been rendered ridiculous, sort of made into baby-dolls, glittering at all costs, covered with gewgaw accessories, loaded with gimmicks and gadgets and bedroom suggestiveness. Which could be fine. But not for working women, whose lives were no different from the lives of men, and who needed to dress for the same purposes: with a basic need for everyday elegance, simplicity. That was my basic idea." Armani ranks with Poiret, who officially freed women from corsets, and with Coco Chanel, who helped strip away crinolines and lace to establish a different form of dignity. Like them, he holds an emblematic position in the history of fashion precisely because he struck a decisive blow on behalf of the aesthetic emancipation of women.

He also—and especially—brought revolution to men's fashion: "As a buyer, I had difficulties because I had to satisfy a type of customer who could spend plenty of money for clothing," he recalls, "but the suits that were available were too stiff, and they made all men look alike. I wanted suits that would emphasize a man's personality and exalt his body. And so, when I went into business for myself, I decided to get rid of all those 'structures' in the jackets. That was what made everyone look alike. I experimented, letting the fabric drape over a man's body, focusing attention on what were usually called 'defects.' The idea was to deconstruct the suit, allowing greater freedom of movement. I believe that this was essential, because it allowed men a more personal, authentic look." The shoulders and the buttons moved downward; the lapels became narrower; the cut, the proportions, and the volumes all changed; the internal structure was radically modified.

At first, his fashion was more popular with artists, actors, and architects, the types of people who could appreciate the new shape of the jackets and understand that a flaw was not necessarily a defect but a virtue: "Since these individuals wore old jackets, old sweaters, and loved them when they were used, and no longer new, they felt a sense of affinity toward my fashion, and I felt that I was one of them." As usual, it was dissatisfaction that drove Giorgio Armani, who hated jackets the way they were. And that dissatisfaction was the basis for the empire he created. Sensing that what was missing, what was needed, was a new nonchalance, an easygoing elegance, he sought an equilibrium between the function of the formal suit—the uniform—and the sensations of adaptability to the body, softness, and relaxation. Deconstructing the men's jacket, giving it an edge of casual relaxation, he created a new style that proved to be a perfect blend of the hippie tradition, with its rejection of all rules and restrictions, and the bourgeois uniform. It was a new and extraordinary mediation: suddenly the elegant drawing room admitted the concept of "lived in," the warmth of the moment. It was exactly what had been missing.

Savorelli recalled: "There was great enthusiasm among the buyers. Paris was experiencing a period of crisis, and so was Dior. Lagerfeld was designing Chloe, and then there was Saint Laurent, who represented the super classic style. There was a need for young blood. We had the ateliers, the workshops, which regularly worked miracles. The French designers had to come to Italy to get their knitwear produced. Sonia Rykiel, who was famous, had her workshop in Vicenza. It was all spontaneous and exciting."

Things happened serendipitously, and encounters between talented individuals produced results that are still valid and surprising today. Such was the case when Giorgio Armani met Flavio Lucchini in the early seventies, when he was the editor in chief of *L'Uomo Vogue*. Lucchini listened to what Giorgio had to say and encouraged him to create a label of his own, urging him to finish an entire collection. (As they were chatting, Flavio cut a few letters from the pages of his magazine and assembled his name; the famous logo of the Giorgio Armani company is a reworking of this simple collage.) Giorgio confessed his doubts, particularly his financial concerns. Flavio replied with friendly reassurance, promising him all the support he could offer. And he matched his words with deeds, introducing Armani to the public in a seven-page layout in *L'Uomo Vogue*, then the principal showcase for men's fashion.

Gisella Borioli, who with Flavio Lucchini was a guiding spirit of the magazine, recalls: "The first time that we did a fashion layout with his creations, we faced the problem of who to use as a model and who to use as a photographer. We were always searching for new photographers, and so we thought of Aldo Fallai, who was sort of well known, and we asked Armani himself to be the model. The photographs were taken in a well-known Milanese café, the Bar Taveggia: Giorgio Armani, dressed in his knitwear and jackets, posed for Aldo Fallai." Thus began a major working relationship: Fallai became Armani's photographer, the first in a succession—Peter Lindbergh, Paolo Roversi, Tom Munro, and Albert Watson—who would immortalize Giorgio's designs over the years.

Current events and fashion were intertwined, and the military style was in the air—it was just after the end of the Vietnam War. So when Oliviero Toscani came back from the United States, where he had done a photo layout using surplus from the U.S. Army, Gisella and Flavio suggested that Armani take the military look as his muse. The idea struck a chord, and he developed an entire collection of clothing inspired by uniforms, ranging from battle jackets to the trousers we all know that now form part of the wardrobe of every boy and young man. It was the invention of a new genre. "Galeotti was also delighted, an enthusiastic supporter of the idea," Gisella continues.

> When we finally had the clothing, we needed to figure out a layout. And we decided that the image of a long-haired guy with a mustache was old. So we decided to seek out healthy, clean-cut, muscular men, to depict a new idea. It was 1977, and we had just bought a house in Corsica. We decided to use soldiers from the island's

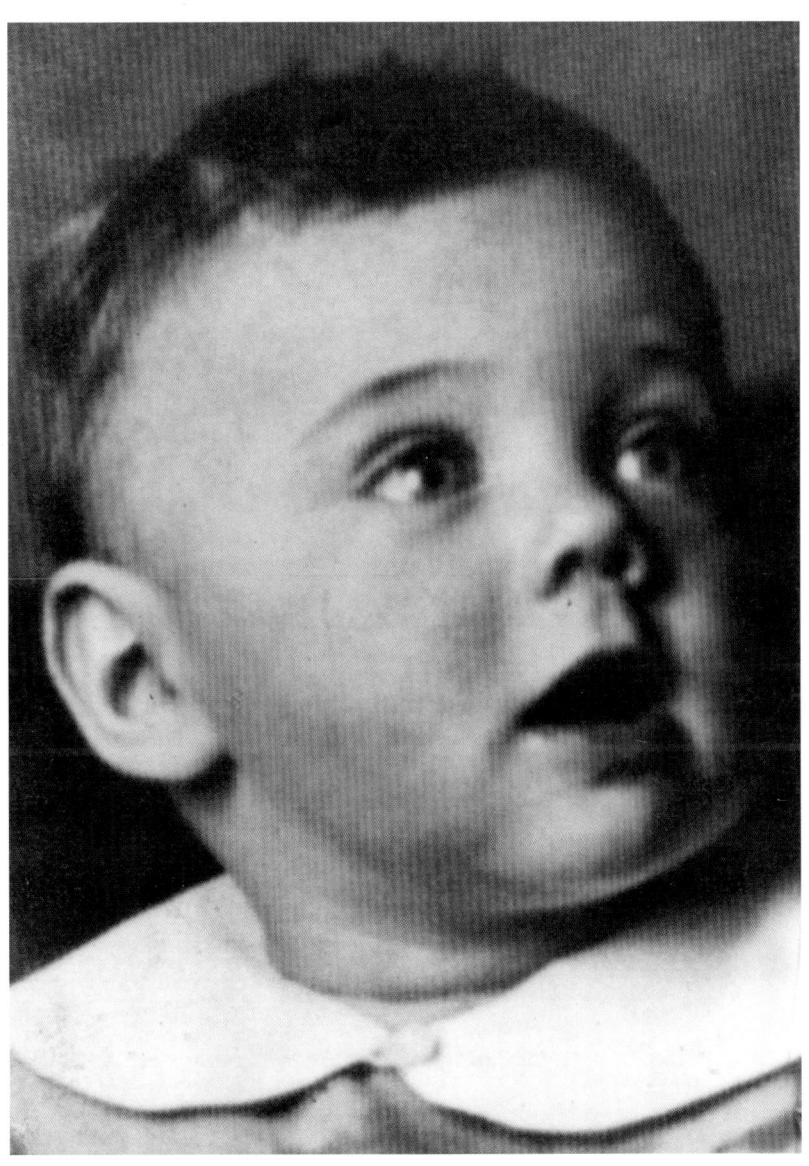

Giorgio Armani at six months.

Top: Giorgio with his mother and brother Sergio on vacation in Riccione in 1937.
Bottom: Giorgio, Rosanna, and Sergio. "Mom liked dressing us the same."
Opposite: Giorgio and his mother at the beach in Riccione.

Top: A Sunday by the river Trebbia.
Bottom: Giorgio with his brother and a friend in the countryside around Rivergaro.

A holiday in the mountains in the 1940s.

Top left: On leave!
Top right: A portrait with his boxer.
Bottom: Sergio, Giorgio, and daddy Armani.
Opposite: Rosanna and Giorgio in the summer of 1955 in Trieste.

Above: Giorgio and Jago.
Opposite, top: A self-portrait.
Opposite, bottom: Giorgio and his mother in Milan in the 1950s.

Top: At Bora Bora in 1982.
Bottom: On the Sicilian island of Pantelleria, in front of his house.
Opposite: In his garden, Pantelleria.

Holidays in Pantelleria.
Top: With friends at the outdoor home bar.
Bottom: Along the road, on a trip to the volcano.

Top: At Lake Venere.
Bottom: Group photo before leaving.

Top: At Jaisalmer (India) in 1995.
Bottom: Tina with Giorgio Armani in the swimming pool at Pantelleria.

On Pantelleria with Lauren Hutton in 1990.
Photo © Isabelle Snyder

Holidays in Pantelleria.
Top: Waiting at the airport.
Bottom: "With Lauren for the usual spin on the motorbike." Photo © Isabelle Snyder

Top. Giorgio Armani with his sister, Rosanna.
Bottom left: With Claudia Cardinale at Lake Venere.
Bottom right: With Ornella Muti.

Top: In the desert close to Jaisalmer (India, 1995.)
Bottom: Jaisalmer (India, 1995).
Opposite, top, both: Silvana and Giorgio Armani shopping in Hammamet (Tunisia).
Opposite, bottom: …and in Kelibia.

Top: In India.
Bottom: At Amber (India).

Top: Andrea Camerana with uncle Giorgio Armani in Bikaner (India).
Bottom: A photo safari around Lake Nakuru (Kenya, 1989).

In the streets of Shanghai.
Photo © Roger Hutchings

Souvenir photo with a young fan in Shanghai.

One of the many weekends at Broni with Poldo and Polly.
Photo © Lord Snowdon

garrison of the Foreign Legion. But a highly amused general told me that he would have to ask permission from the French Ministry of Defense. Too much trouble. We went back to Milan, and I started to take a look at Italian soldiers. In the end we received permission from the Perrucchetti barracks, which is where we went to do the layout. Giorgio came along with Fallai, and a number of real soldiers plus a few models that Aldo brought along. It was really revolutionary; we proposed an image of a clean, healthy man wearing these new clothes. The layout appeared in the June–July issue of L'Uomo Vogue for 1977. I think that all this helped to inspire Sergio Galeotti to create Emporio Armani. He got the idea from the spirit of the layout, from the military medals, from the heavy shirts and jackets. After this project, Giorgio Armani received a couple of requests from the Italian navy and army to design their uniforms.

Success came quickly. The company, founded with capital of 10 million lire (roughly $10,000) in 1975, earned 80 million lire (roughly $80,000) with its first menswear collection and 30 million lire (roughly $30,000) with the first womenswear collection. Just one year later, its turnover increased to 569 million lire (over $500,000); ten years later, in 1985, it had swollen to 291 billion lire, about $300 million).

The Americans came knocking, too. Fred Pressman, president of the luxury department store Barneys, in New York, was the first to grasp the potential of Armani's fashion for the U.S. market. Pressman worked with Armani in an office barely twelve feet square, with nothing but a few wicker chairs set around a huge worktable that was used interchangeably for long business meetings, press conferences, and frugal meals: "I purchased an Armani collection in a small hotel, where the only light came from a lamp that was so dim you couldn't see the colors. Armani had to take the lampshade off." He remembers, "The manufacturers told me that I was ruining the industry, by promoting rumpled and wrinkled cloth. They couldn't manage to see the collection in terms of lifestyle, but only in terms of good or bad fashion. They couldn't understand that people might want articles of clothing that rumpled in just this way or dropped in just that manner." Thanks to his determination, however, the same year he introduced Armani's fashion in the United States—1976—the combined sales for both lines reached $90,000. Just six years later, the U.S. turnover had grown to $24 million. "America understood the importance of Giorgio Armani before anyone else," writes Natalia Aspesi, "because it was a country with a pioneering spirit, where women suddenly found themselves in the workplace where they needed a new kind of armor." They needed clothing suitable for the office, but they wanted it to be attractive, too. Armani understood the new demand his fashion fulfilled, stating in an interview with an Italian magazine, talking about his jackets: "I really do hope that they have given women a tone of relaxed confidence and the healthy sensation of being invulnerable," adding that he further hoped the women who wore his clothes felt a little safer from the leering impertinence of men.

Armani was well aware of the importance of the fashion press. Beppe Modenese recalls:

> I believe that Galeotti helped him here as well; they tell me that he immediately invested heavily in his image. If

he earned a thousand, he'd spend five hundred on his image, on full-page ads in the press. Dating from that period was, in my opinion, a meeting that was very important to him, which I think most people know nothing about. Sergio Galeotti was working with Larius Miani, and that was how he met Renato Della Valle, a real estate agent who was very successful at the time, a young, likable, enthusiastic guy. Miani had recommended investing money in fashion. And for a short time he became a partner, along with Miani, with Armani and Galeotti. Renato, who was a very generous individual, owned a small private plane, and he suggested: "Invite all the fashion journalists that you like, and take them wherever you want." He opened the doors for Giorgio to a world he had known nothing about. I believe that he was the one who persuaded Giorgio and Sergio to move to the Via Durini, which was a great idea, because it catapulted them head and shoulders above all the rest.

Sure enough, it wasn't long before the company had to expand its offices, and, after a brief stay in a studio in the Via Santa Cecilia, the courageous—and intelligent—decision was made to move to the main floor of the prestigious Palazzo Durini Caproni di Taliedo, a handsome eighteenth-century building designed by the architect Francesco Maria Richini, at number 24 on the Via Durini, right in the heart of Milan. The rooms are adorned with mythological and allegorical frescoes done by Nuvoloni, Crespi, and Schusters, local painters from the period who also did the gold-leaf decorations on the doors and the boiseries. Setting up shop in this palazzo proved to be a strategic choice that immediately increased the prestige of the Giorgio Armani company, making a favorable impression on the press and buyers alike. Franco Savorelli remembers: "Sergio was very attentive to this sort of issue, and he was very sensitive. He required the buyers—and the Americans found this to be scandalous—and the American department stores that attended to make a small order, sight unseen; this was in part to prevent them from coming and copying, as they often did. Remember, in America whole pages would come out in the fashion magazines, and the captions would read 'Here is a jacket just like the one made by the great Italian designer' and that was just what they did, they would imitate Italian style." The palazzo in the Via Durini was also a great location for parties, as Savorelli recalled: "The Festa d'Oro, or Feast of Gold. It was 1976, and it was one of the most exclusive social events in Milan in the period. Giorgio's idea—and of course, I had a role in coming up with this one—was to hold a party in honor of Santa Lucia, St. Lucy's eve, the longest night of the year. It was a revolution for the time: the entire floor of the Palazzo Durini was covered with gold, there was a triumph of gold-covered pineapples, there were ottomans, cushions, an incredible buffet. All of the leading citizens of Milan were fighting to get an invitation; for years it was the talk of the town. We even invited the Sorelle Bandiera [a drag group from Italian television]." There was a furious argument because their show was supposed to last half an hour, but Galeotti put his foot down and absolutely prohibited anything longer than ten minutes, instinctively honoring one of the fundamental laws of modern communications: speed.

In the midseventies, the oil crunch led to a major crisis in the Italian textile and apparel market. At the time, a young scion of the Turinese industrial aristocracy, Marco Rivetti, had just begun working in the family company, Gruppo Finanziario Tessile (GFT), as director of the womenswear division, under the Cori label. In 1975 GFT was "monolithic and single-product," Rivetti said. "We made jackets that all looked the same, for men and women, with the Facis and Cori labels. But the market had changed and labor costs were rising. We needed a new strategy: either we needed to aim at a low target, manufacturing jeans for 2 thousand lire [about $2] a pair less than Jesus Jeans and emphasizing the advertising and promotion, or else aiming at a high target." GFT had purchased a factory that made outerwear and had a contract with the couturier Emanuel Ungaro, and Rivetti sensed that such relationships between fashion and manufacturing could constitute a turning point for the sector: adding fashion to industrial production just might be the way out of crisis. Carlo Rivetti—a cousin of Marco's and the owner of C. P. Company—recalled: "It was pure chance: Marco got a phone call from Milan suggesting that he go meet a young man and his partner; they were experiencing a financial crisis because their business had been growing too quickly. They were doing so well that they couldn't keep up with things." That is how Sergio Galeotti explained the fortuitous pairing with GFT: "When we reached a turnover of 2 billion lire [about $2 million], I understood that we could no longer survive on our own, in terms of finance and in terms of organization."

Armani had already presented three collections with great success. "At the time, we could have purchased the Giorgio Armani company," Carlo Rivetti went on. "Instead, we decided, in part out of respect, to purchase the fabric warehouse. That gave the company a financial cushion. Later, we started paying for the collections as well. They were incredible years.

This was the birth of what in Italy we call *'il made in Italy'*; we didn't even have terms for the new ideas, at least in Italian. We didn't think of ourselves as *licenziatari* or *licenzianti* [licensers], or of Armani as a *stilista* [designer]; we never talked about licenses at all. I remember Armani's legendary lawyer, together with the lawyer Ugona, the in-house GFT counsel, inventing the various words that identified the roles. It was just an explosive beginning." Soon changes were made in the sales system.

> We had always sold with single-label agents, who had a little van, a suitcase, and an array of samples. Galeotti told us that it was an outmoded way of doing business, and that we needed to open a showroom (I don't know if he already used the English term). We persuaded our best agent, Sanzo Zappieri, to move from Turin to Milan. Armani selected the space, furnished it (it wasn't far from the Via Durini), and we invented, almost against our will, a new way of selling. Galeotti's idea was to force the clients to move: "We'll bring them inside our world, we'll show them our entire universe." And it was also a way of saying: we aren't coming to see you anymore, now you have to come see us. It was a powerful way of showing who was in charge. And it worked beautifully. During the third season, Saks Fifth Avenue became a client. We took special pains to deliver that first order in the best way imaginable. The clothes arrived and they were all sold in a week, the best-selling item in the entire department store. The same thing happened for the second and third season, in bigger and bigger quantities.

Of course, none of this could have happened without publicity. As Carlo Rivetti acknowledges, "The press played a role, thanks to young fashion journalists such as Adriana Mulassano, Natalia Aspesi, and Pia Soli. The dailies, before that, never covered fashion. Then they realized that fashion was fashionable. An era was dawning."

Armani was a major asset for GFT, and not only because his clothing sold so remarkably well: he brought prestige and technical knowledge to the entire company. "I remember Giorgio Armani's first visit," Carlo Rivetti said as he continued his story.

> He came to the Settimo plant near Turin, where on the ground floor we used to "decapizzare" our fabrics, putting them through a hot, boiling steam-treatment, which stabilized the fabric, but at the cost of much of its softness. At the time, Armani used really innovative fabrics, very loose and flowing. When he saw that department, he said, "You don't do that to my fabrics." And of course, we didn't, and the first collection we produced was extremely popular. Armani had a remarkable talent. He did things that were fundamental, in technical terms as well. Not only did he reinvent the men's jacket, he found new ways of using fabrics, especially in those years, with astonishing, innovative color treatments. The first collection we produced was spectacularly successful, but three weeks later we had to take back about 70 percent of the production, because the items weren't holding together. We still lacked the technology to keep up with Armani's creativity. At the time, the apparel

textiles sector wasn't very well organized, and the product lacked consumer appeal. Italy didn't have much of an industrial reputation.

According to textile manufacturer Vittorio Solbiati, Armani was "like Giorgetto Giugiaro: innovative in forms and products." He knew what an industrial manufacturing process could yield, and he stimulated his colleagues to do things they wouldn't have achieved otherwise. Marco Rivetti realized that the work Armani was doing was waking up the industry, prompting the staff in the technical side of production to use their imaginations. Carlo Rivetti said:

> GFT was a major manufacturing concern, and young Marco had invented something new. The effect was spectacular, though the old-timers looked at it all with a degree of suspicion. In the Piedmontese industrial structure, organized according to a pyramidal hierarchy, the driving forces were loyalty and seniority. Suddenly, in the midst of that structure, a new variable was introduced: fashion, a soft variable, hard to quantify. It was an overwhelming cultural shock. And it was especially astonishing to see the changes that occurred in the womenswear division where they were working on Giorgio Armani creations: the way they dressed, their attitudes, were different from the usual industrial setting. They were proud to work for Giorgio Armani. It was fantastic.

Here is what Marco Rivetti said in an interview a few years after he began working with Armani:

In the company, the organization of labor has changed in part. We still work on an assembly line, we're still paid by the piece. But we have had to diversify our machinery: doing certain things requires new machinery. And the skilled work changed. Turin is a city of seamstresses, and we have a supremely talented staff. But the worker who stitches an Armani jacket will now do a better job of stitching a Cori jacket. The pattern cutters who transpose sketches onto cardboard work for both the Armani label and for others. And of course, they don't copy. But they wind up using, wherever possible, the same finishing methods, the same specific techniques. All of our production is improving. Italian fashion owes a great deal to these artisanal skills, which Germany intentionally scattered to the winds and which France chose to ignore.

Where France had decided that the textiles and apparel sector was no longer strategic and needed to be dismantled, Italy, whose textile industry continued to be an important part of the economy, nurtured a generation of remarkable fashion designers, such as Krizia, Walter Albini, and Armani. Concluded Carlo Rivetti, "If there had been no oil crisis, then perhaps this industry wouldn't have opened their doors to them."

CHAPTER FOUR

Discovering America

For Italian designers, the late seventies heralded a boom. "I'm now ready for the challenge; I'm daring to take my creations into the lion's den. I'm opening up shops in the Faubourg St. Honoré, the center of high fashion, and in St. Germain, the section of Paris where the artists live," Armani told an interviewer in 1979. That year, for the first time, total business revenue during Milan's prêt-à-porter fashion shows was greater than the corresponding turnover in Paris. Fashion became a topic of study for sociologists: Francesco Alberoni found that Italian creativity enjoyed a clear superiority. Liberated from their deep-rooted inferiority complex with regard to the French, Italian designers and manufacturers began in these years their long and momentous climb to prominence, a status that the Italians describe with the terms *Il Made in Italy* and *Sistema* (referring to the Italian fashion system).

In just a few short years, Armani surged out of the discreet realm of professional recognition to the dizzying heights of international stardom. On April 4, 1978, in Hollywood, Diane Keaton accepted her Best Actress Oscar for her role in Woody Allen's *Annie Hall* wearing an Armani jacket. Armani was now an established name, and everyone knew it. Among his clients was Paola Ruffo, Princess of Liège, a leading member of the jet set and the future queen of Belgium. Other famous clients were

Michelangelo Antonioni and Camilla Cederna, a prominent Italian journalist renowned for her integrity. The Armani jacket became a full-fledged status symbol. John Travolta, whose first moment of major stardom came in the late seventies with his hits *Saturday Night Fever* and *Grease*, visited the Giorgio Armani atelier in Milan to select some forty suits that would be part of the wardrobe for *American Gigolo* (1980), in which he was supposed to star. (Travolta's manager, Bob Le Mond—already a passionate Armani fan—had persuaded director Paul Schrader that this new Italian style would work effectively in the movie.) But Travolta made the fatal misstep of turning down the role (opting instead to star in *Urban Cowboy*), and the part went to Richard Gere, costarring with Lauren Hutton—who would in time become a close friend and frequent spokesperson for Armani.

Not only did the movie mark the beginning of Richard Gere's ascent to the status of a sex symbol and male icon of the eighties, it had consequences that went well beyond the realm of film. Perhaps most influential was the famous scene in which Gere chooses his outfit for the evening. Moving to the rhythm of a driving beat, he selects his ensemble with scientific precision from among his considerable array of jackets, shirts, and ties in a hitherto-unseen palette of harmonious colors. It was an image that became a billboard for the Armani style. The shadiness of the leading character was not just tempered by the confidently consistent aesthetic of his clothing, it was even ennobled to some extent. The suits, the accessories, the entire look belonged to an entirely new visual language. The shoulders—broad yet not stiff—the narrow lapels and waist, the softness of the fabrics, and the sense of restrained indulgence in the tailoring, all perfectly expressed the idea of sensuality: "It was like looking at an old carpet in which the natural colors blend and fade," Gere commented, "unlike what happens with these new carpets made with synthetic fibers, in which the colors are uniform." Gere went on to say: "I don't know any other designers."

Diana Ross, Donna Summer, Lauren Bacall, Monica Vitti, Dustin Hoffman, Jack Nicholson, and Franco Nero: the list grew longer and longer from this point forward. Yet Armani rejected the label of designer to the stars: "I like to create clothing for people who work, and that includes actors and actresses, inasmuch as they are people who work, and not just as stars. I don't want to become a dictator who imposes his likes and dislikes at all costs. I don't believe that fashion should be a form of slavery. Wearing clothing should, however, be fun and reassuring, a way of feeling comfortable and confident," he said. Whatever the case, he soon came to understand the axiom "With success comes responsibility." He himself admitted that life had been a lot more fun just a few years before, when the company, under Galeotti's management, was still self-financing and its clients were relatively few, though prestigious and international—let's not forget that Armani suits were already being sold in the strategic outlets in New York and London. "But now I have twenty days' vacation a year, like any other office worker; I work twelve hours a day, because this is a profession that demands everything from you." In that period, the burgeoning Armani empire was governed by just five people: Giorgio, who designed the collections and supervised the public image; Sergio Galeotti, who oversaw the commercial side of the business; Marisa Bulleghin, Armani's assistant; Adriano Giannelli, who was in charge of the international market; and Cesare Giorgino, who supervised the menswear collections. Giorgio's tendency to centralize, to refuse to delegate, was a powerful personality trait, and work was an integral part of his life, to the point that the professional invariably mingled with the personal. Armani's routine in this period was anything but exciting. Every morning at nine o'clock, he entered his office in the Via Durini. He spent his short holidays in his house in Cala di Levante on the island of Pantelleria, invariably in August, just when the big factories in the north of Italy shut down for the summer break. He had an apartment in the center of Milan, in the Via Santa Cecilia, which he himself decorated and furnished. He lived there with Galeotti; Gigi, his faithful nine-year-old bulldog; and Sun Valley, more familiarly known as Micio, a magnificent blue Persian cat. A housekeeper kept the place clean and orderly. Armani didn't smoke, he drank very little, and he ate with restraint, even though there are those who say that he can never resist a plate of authentic northern Italian salami. He loved *anolini piacentini* and roast chicken. He disliked socializing, and, as now, he was extremely neat. His wardrobe even then was very spare. He loved dark blue trousers and Lacoste shirts, though he would soon replace these with his legendary dark blue T-shirts, short- or long-sleeved: a minimalist uniform that would contribute to the construction of the image of sober yet luxurious consistency that everyone associates with Giorgio Armani.

One year, Armani and Galeotti were guests of Beppe Modenese in Monte Marcello, and the host still vividly recalls how fresh was Armani's view of the world, how cheerfully he embraced new experience: "Our house was all black and white," Modenese recalls, "and Giorgio loved it. We had a sailboat, too, a Castellammare *gozzo*. We took a sail in the Gulf of La Spezia, a beautiful, romantic place, and I remember that he would say to Sergio, see, I want this . . . and I want that. He was captivated by everything he saw."

Right after that, in 1978, Armani and Galeotti bought their villa in Forte dei Marmi, near where Sergio was born; it would be one of the houses that Giorgio would use for short holidays or on weekends.

That same year, he started a more affordable line, which he named Le Collezioni, and a few years after he signed a licensing agreement with L'Oréal for perfumes. But Armani's major relationship with the United States was consolidated with the foundation in 1979 of the Giorgio Armani Men's Wear Corporation USA in partnership with GFT and with the hiring of Gabriella Forte by the Giorgio Armani company.

The talented New York manager joined Giorgio Armani as vice president for operations and soon grew to be an important figure within the organization. In charge of operations in the United States, press relations, marketing, and events, Forte was tireless. Dubbed the "terrible terrier" for her determination, she was widely feared: there are stories of staff members in tears, sobbing in bathrooms or weeping openly in the hallway. For the fifteen long years she worked alongside Armani's sister, Rosanna—who came to work for the corporation a few years later—the two formed a redoubtable barrier protecting the Giorgio Armani company from the outside world. Though they both had strong personalities, which led to frequent clashes, their rivalry did nothing but contribute to the growth of the Armani myth, adding to its aura of magic and discouraging liberties with its image.

Gabriella Forte played a decisive role in creating links between Armani and the world of film. Nowadays, of course, every designer vies to dress the stars of Hollywood, but for many years their wardrobes were the exclusive territory of Giorgio Armani. He was the first Italian designer to attract a genuine international following. The *New York Times* ran an article about him, and a special report was broadcast on American television. "All modesty aside, I have come here to tell American men how to dress," the designer told a leading Italian weekly. "The time is right, America is ready. On university campuses, on ranches, and in the suburbs, people may still choose to wear jeans, T-shirts, and sports shirts. But you need only take a stroll through downtown New York, or even venture further out, into the suburbs where former New Yorkers now live, and you will see that living elegantly is something that Americans like as well. It's just a matter of calibrating their willingness, in other words, adjusting the sights of their taste, which has been evolving for years."

In 1979 Armani received the Neiman Marcus Award in the United States. The prize was established in 1938 by Stanley Marcus—the president of the Neiman Marcus chain of department stores—to acknowledge the creative talents that distinguished themselves in various fields, from design and advertising to craftsmanship and fashion. It is a sort of fashion Oscar, and few Italian designers had ever won it: the Missonis in 1973; Emilio Pucci, Roberta di Camerino, and Mirsa in the fifties. In that same period, Saks Fifth Avenue asked Armani to hold a trunk show in New York, a type of presentation normally restricted to the best customers of a given department store, that was very popular in the United States at the time. A new era was dawning. Carlo Rivetti was an eyewitness to Armani's first show in the United States:

> It was held on the top floor, at seven in the evening, after the store closed. That was my first trip to America, and I think it was Giorgio's first trip as well. I still remember,

we flew economy, because we had no money. The show was at seven in the evening, as I said, but there was already a line at six. And there's nothing like people standing in line to attract more people, curious about what's happening. We expected four hundred people, but there were four thousand. This was truly the birth of what the Italians call *"Il Made in Italy."* No one expected it. Across from Saks were the empty offices of the Shah of Iran. Saks took all the displays over there, and in the days that followed, more shows were held to satisfy the customers. There were no strategies, no planning, only the power of this one man.

For the party celebrating the success of the presentation at Saks, Armani and Galeotti rented Studio 54, the legendary New York discotheque among whose regular clientele could be found Truman Capote, Elizabeth Taylor, Andy Warhol, and Elton John. The club had witnessed eccentricities of every sort, including a spectacular entrance by Bianca Jagger riding a white horse during her thirtieth birthday party. Galeotti and Armani transformed it completely: everything was pale and peculiar—the outfits worn by the musicians, the wallpaper, the pillars, and the various facilities—every detail canceled yet underscored by a sea of white; a blend of Great Gatsby and a Martin Margiela *ante litteram*, the setting was timeless and surreal, luxuriant and dreamy. With the brilliant direction of Armani and Galeotti, the discotheque became a theater, and the dance floor was invaded by the classic dancers of the Trockadero Ballet—all of them transvestites—in a light-hearted juxtaposition of romanticism and modernity. Then the orchestra began to play, first Tchaikovsky's *Swan Lake* and then *The*

Nutcracker Suite, and the ballerinos, in a swirl of tutus and crinolines, began to pirouette in the temple of disco music, to the enthusiastic applause of the privileged few who had been invited to attend.

The press of the period reported that "Armani seemed Louis XIV." The evening's entertainment, which was considered one of the most spectacular and exclusive social events of its day, not only highlighted Giorgio Armani's personal success; it also modernized the image of Italy. Turning its back on the gray and long-suffering imagery of neorealism through the filter of which Americans were accustomed to viewing it, Italy adopted a set of entirely opposing ideals: elegance, glamour, and confidence, a sense of stylistic superiority that has never been questioned since. From the perception of Italy as the source of demoralized, ignorant immigrants, cardboard suitcases in hand, the vision shifted to a triumph of beauty and creative power. The media waxed eloquent on the nation's taste and style and printed paeans to the brilliant achievements of the developing fashion industry. In the April 1979 issue of *L'Uomo Vogue*, Matthew Serra, head buyer for Saks Fifth Avenue, called Armani "the Michelangelo of fashion," stating that Armani had created the perfect silhouette that everyone wanted to imitate. In 1980 Andy Warhol invited Giorgio Armani to appear on his television program, *Andy Warhol's TV*, where he was interviewed by the brilliant Italian journalist Daniela Morera. For years the rhapsodies Armani provoked were unstoppable, perhaps comparable only to the later wave of excitement generated by Romeo Gigli. His name would be mentioned in the same breath as Picasso's. Fashion journalists would launch into moist-eyed panegyrics of praise after every show, smugly commiserating, "I'm so sorry you missed it, you would have understood so much," whenever they met a colleague from a lesser publication who had not enjoyed the privilege of attending the unveiling of the latest miracle. Increasingly moving away from the cliché of the Bel Paese, land of mandolins, Italy became a player in the Great Game.

Armani's talent lies in his ability to understand society, and the width of his lapels and the sobriety of his fashion represent much more than an application of the golden mean. Instinctively inclined toward harmony, obsessed with aesthetics, Armani intuited the full potential of fashion, calling attention to the cultural and sociological attributes of the field. He did so not with words but with actions, by designing and cutting, setting forth and communicating to the world a style that was sober and rigorous yet soft and very thirties in look and feel amid the loud arugula-ridden atmosphere of the eighties. He ignored the uproar that had ruffled the minds of consumers during the previous decade and, punctual as a precision timepiece, offered new aesthetic options for a return to fashion.

In that postrevolutionary atmosphere that was about to hurl itself lemminglike into joie de vivre, it was easy to confound lightheartedness with superficiality. The eighties were prolix and arrogant, so colorful and spectacular that they inevitably had to fade to black. They were years of infinite potential, of the yuppie and Reaganesque hedonism, of the rapid growth of Milan and of idiotic kneejerk catchphrases. Of plastic and vying for power. The world witnessed the triumph of the manager. Two-dimensionality and shallowness became values, emptiness became an admired quality. It was a time of aesthetic enthusiasm, of the rediscovery of an elastic, shifting morality, a time of confusion in which everything became plausible. The air was filled with the notes of Duran Duran's "Wild Boys" and the melodies of Michael Jackson, whose makeup and gold lamé outfits made artifice acceptable for men, undercutting all pride in affiliation and identity: as long as there was success, nothing else mattered. With the death of John Lennon on December 8, 1980, a page turned symbolically: from the frenetic pursuit of light, of clear and unattainable harmony, that had transfixed an entire generation, the world fell into a harsh, self-indulgent pragmatism, accompanied by the siren song of fashion and dominated by a creeping cynicism.

Madonna, who was then a platinum blonde, would soon show the world that it is possible to be petite and none too attractive, with an average voice, and still become a famous singer and a role model to the world. Communication supplanted content. Bobby McFerrin sang "Don't Worry, Be Happy," and one brand name was Think Pink. Jane Fonda pranced around dressed in tiny fuchsia and china blue leotards and fluorescent legwarmers, creating converts to the religion of aerobics. The Fiorucci adhesives, which in time became collectibles, would help spread an idea of carefree life that was expressed through an impressive spectrum of chromatic exuberance. Seen from a distance, from on high, from a hypothetical Martian spaceship, society must have looked happy. These were years of folly, discotheques, euphoria glittering with sequins; years of cocaine, rivers of cash, wretched waste and excess; a nomadic social free-for-all focused obsessively on appearance. But they were also the years of a laborious post-terrorism reconstruction. And at the end of the breathless race lay AIDS.

This intense period saw, on the one hand, Thatcherism and the Falklands War and, on the other, glittering runway presentations, the punks in Kings Road, and the first New York graffiti artists. The image of fashion was gradually consolidated, becoming something other, something more. It erupted beyond the accepted borders and took on the trappings of a genuine psychological strategy, founded on a cult of personality and the spread of a mission. The armies were dressed in shocking pink, orange, and acid green cocktail suits. The uniforms had designer logos and monograms, and feminine authority was expressed through immense shoulder pads: just think back to the exaggerations of Thierry Mugler, Claude Montana, and Jean Paul Gaultier. Side slits and an emphasis on bodies reembraced a concept of sensuality that respected ancient parameters: Barbie came back into fashion. The notion of the top model became current again, an ideal of woman whose beauty was overwhelming, surreal, rendered even more unattainable by a mythology that grew in intricacy and depth with each season, abetted by the photographs of Bill King, Herb Ritts, Patrick Demarchelier, Richard Avedon, and Irving Penn and movies such as *The Woman in Red* and *Nine and a Half Weeks*.

It was a decade in which everything happened: everything that exists in fashion as we understand it today is in a certain sense a development from or a reaction to everything that was produced in those years. And it was Italy that set the pace, giving a new meaning to the word *fashion* and endowing it with an unmistakable coloring, an imprint engendered by such significant personalities as the Missonis, who went far beyond the *Munsell Book of Color* to invent a visual language with its own lines and color formulas that even today remains a unique achievement. Another such personality was Gianni Versace, Giorgio Armani's great rival, who imagined florid, cheerful women, multicolor prints, and pop paintings reproduced on fabric, applying a principle of freedom in color combinations the likes of which only Emilio Pucci had dared to match before him.

Enrico Coveri, too, helped to enliven the scene with his luminescent little outfits, made with 101 contrasting strips and glittering with sequins and colorful plastic disks. And then Franco Moschino appeared, assigning new meaning to Italy's tricolor flag, transforming it into a logo, an indelible, youthful emblem, even a source of humor.

These were flashy, garish, overcharged, unforgettable years, and Giorgio Armani, who had done such an impressive job of introducing new meaning to the Italian image, elegantly freeing it from its past, moved through the crowd like a monarch, confident and serene, surrounded by hordes of proud fans. He went his own way, propelled by the wave of new excitement yet at the same time removed from it, denaturing it with his delicate colors and his unrivaled way of translating exoticism, making use of the lines and styles of other cultures, memories of trips he had taken in reality or only in his imagination, to produce fashion that was sober and comfortable, very European yet embracing the world. Cleaving steadfastly to his own style, he ignored the semantic and ethical turmoil that was raging all around him.

The decade's excess cast a dark shadow, broad and ever expanding, a clear question mark hanging over all the merry confusion reminiscent of nothing so much as a fireworks display at a village festival. Colors began to take on a very specific ideological content within the youth movements, even if over time the nuances of interpretation became increasingly subtle. The electric colors of punk, along with studs, black leather, and plaid, became a spectacularly and deliberately transgressive body of provocation. The so-called dark style, in contrast, was a more introverted form of expression, a radical evocation of the voluntary rejection of the outside world and the disquiet of a period that was once again negotiating the issues of atomic energy in the wake of the devastating nuclear disaster at Chernobyl. It represented an awareness of the social uncertainty that was attempting to distract itself with the carefree colors of glossy magazines.

The euphoric wave of color and invention that swept that decade was also identified with the expressive force of graffiti artists. The urban landscape was suddenly enlivened by the work of artists some known, such as Rammellzee, some of them never to be identified. The walls of the world began to take on color through graffiti art, a frontier art form not least because the conquest of the spaces to be decorated was in and of itself a daring deed. Here, too, color contrasted with the shadows evident in the art, such as Richard Hambleton's, that adorned the walls of a New York that was increasingly and avowedly a place of contradictions and full ferment. Ranged against that darkness emblematic of clandestine, indelible fears stood the hypercolorful humanoids of Keith Haring. Haring's represented the most telling sensibility of the period, perhaps the most interesting aspect of the decade. His art became the logo of the eighties. His compositions of radiant babies and barking dogs are his most popular, but all his work is riddled with a curious sense of humor. Ever since his debut, when he was filling the unused billboard panels of the New York subway system with simple and ironic images, Haring had always made color his standard: "Liveliness is attractive, colors differentiate and define identities."

In sum, the eighties were brightly colored years, from both a visual and a cultural point of view. And at a time when art galleries were opening their doors to artists of color, such as Jean-Michel Basquiat, Benetton launched its multiethnic campaigns, by Oliviero Toscani. But the episode that changed the very nature of runway presentations came in 1980: Giorgio

Armani decided to abandon the Milan Fair, instead holding the runway presentation for the spring-summer collection at his own venue. A caprice? Ingratitude? An affirmation of power? The gesture provoked its share of debate; indeed, it is the subject of disagreement even now. When journalists quizzed him on the reasons for the shift, Armani explained in an unruffled manner:

> Let's just say that runway presentations are just not the ideal medium with which to show the media the things that I have created; runway presentations have become distorted. They are now just huge performances, and they are a way for directors to get paid a lot of money. Where what seems to prevail is the spectacular effect, even if there is no corresponding commercial return. They don't really matter. In the end no one understands a thing, and even the press is disoriented. And in many cases, certain collections aren't matched by a serious industrial reality. I have chosen to hold my own runway presentation in my space in the Via Durini, even if there isn't all that much room. It seats two hundred people. I held two presentations and so I showed my collection to the four hundred people I care about most.

This was a time of change and experimentation for Armani, and two collections stand out as atypical. The first one, for autumn-winter 1981–1982, was based on the paintings of Utamaro, although many believed that the real inspiration was Akira Kurosawa's 1980 movie *Kagemusha*. The collection presented an elaborate array of Japanese imagery, from armor-style corsets to traditional prints, with forays into the world of comics. The other collection was surprising in its sudden and astonishing use of decisive colors and more feminine shapes, inspired by American quilts.

Armani proved to be unfailingly attentive to small shifts in taste and social phenomena. Along with Sergio Galeotti, he realized that the sudden growth of the fashion sector, the overcrowding of the runway presentations and shop windows, was going to boomerang. The burgeoning excess of everything—clothing, images, fashion designers—was chasing away some of the traditional consumers of fashion. There was an allergic reaction to ideas new for their own sake. "At the time, we had opened a small shop right across the street from our offices in the Via Durini," Armani reported,

> and there we began to experiment with menswear collections made primarily in denim. It was called Emporio Armani, and it targeted a younger audience, with less purchasing power, more closely linked to the world of casual wear. I personally supervised the design of the display windows, and the people on the other side of the glass would tell me if I had done a good job . . . but they were especially excited to see the "great designer" of luxury fashion working to bring the same fashion to the less wealthy as well. The content of the fashion was still in keeping with the Armani style, but at lower prices. Immediately, going against the advice of marketing experts of the period, we expanded the collection to include womenswear, creating a line intended for a sector that until then had been the domain of extremely commercial productions, strictly department store. The eagle was conceived in a very spontaneous manner,

when we tried to think of something that would fly high. And it immediately flew high. I liked the eagle just fine, but I wasn't sure about my monogram on it, since I had always been a little finicky about the excessive use of monograms in the world of fashion, for instance, the craze for initials everywhere, from belt buckles to overcoat linings, and then taking them from the lining to the exterior, using it as a decoration on the clothing itself. The problem was the growing phenomenon of copies, which were increasingly common. The imitators were really good at it. Sometimes I fall for it myself, and I would really have to look closely to see whether something was by me. We needed a logo, even if it did not constitute a foolproof deterrent.

And so, once again, an important addition to the immense Armani constellation sprang from something midway between a market analysis and an impulsive gesture. The origin of the new logo was a sketch depicting a fairly realistic, unstylized drawing of an eagle in flight, intended for a series of summer T-shirts. The design was then revised and corrected by Giorgio himself, and it turned into a graphic element: "Its final appearance grew out of a couple of sketches I did on my notepad, between phone calls." Casual though this inception may be, a list of the objects and symbols that characterized the twentieth century would certainly include the Emporio Armani bomber jacket, with its unmistakable symbol, which soon appeared on the backs of young men at all the latitudes of the earth, broadening Armani's horizons but shrinking those of the world.

The first Emporio Armani opened in 1981, the same year Giorgio won the *GQ* Men's Style Award as best designer and the Cutty Sark Award for the International Top Men's Fashion Designer. And though Armani Junior and Armani Jeans were inaugurated, launched in Italy, and eventually introduced in America, it was with Emporio Armani that the popularity of the brand reached its apex. In just two years there were ninety Emporio Armani shops scattered throughout Italy. Giorgio Armani's popularity was growing steadily. Andy Warhol, in touch with the spirit of the times and a tireless hunter of icons, even painted his portrait.

"I met him [Armani] between 1981 and 1982," recalls Patrick McCarthy, who was then the European editor of *W* in Paris and is now the chairman and editorial director of Fairchild Publications. "A very young Gini Alhadeff, who was his assistant at the time, introduced me to him. The palazzo in the Via Durini made quite an impression on me. The first thing that came to mind was that he was a shy man, but very strong, with a great sense of humor." McCarthy, who immediately became a close friend of Armani's, recalls Sergio Galeotti as an exceptionally funny and mischievous person, very unconventional. "I spent time in the maisons of Yves Saint Laurent and Givenchy and I wasn't used to people like this, with a new vision of fashion. Even though they had this immense palazzo, they were like two revolutionaries: both in the way they showed their clothing and in the style of the clothing itself. They had a spontaneity that didn't exist in Paris at the time."

Giorgio Armani's empire grew out of a specific ethos, which has never shown signs of wavering: personal attention to shifts in society but also to the slightest details. Even now, you can find him in the Via Manzoni, attracting the startled gazes of the locals and the flashes of the astonished Japanese, personally checking the effect of the display windows of his megastore.

It is an odd dichotomy: on the one hand, there is the unreachable Armani, protected by his loyal colleagues who dig deeper and deeper moats around the castle and erect ever higher, more impregnable walls, thus feeding the old Louis XIV image, while, on the other hand, we find the more familiar, classic Armani, the exacting and tireless worker and attentive, concerned shopkeeper, "close to the ordinary people," as he puts it himself.

In 1982 Sergio Galeotti, with Giorgio's approval, asked Rosanna Armani to come work for the company: "Why don't you quit working for magazines and come oversee advertising and photography?" This is how Rosanna describes her transition to the Giorgio Armani company. "I was working at *Playboy Italia* at the time, as a photo editor, with Oreste del Buono. Before that I worked at *Annabella* as a fashion editor. I was happy that the offer came from Galeotti, in part because Giorgio would have had a hard time asking me, and in fact probably never would." Rosanna accepted the offer and embraced the spirit of the company, taking part in meetings and acting as liaison with the Camera della Moda (Chamber of Fashion). For twenty years, she would supervise the advertising and publicity and communications campaigns. "All of the campaigns from the beginning of the eighties to the midnineties were overseen by Rosanna," according to Adriana Mulassano, a major journalist for the *Corriere della Sera*. Giorgio would critique the campaigns and decide which photograph would be the picture of the season, "but she supervised the work from A to Z, taking great care to follow the exact brief, but also with a genius that Giorgio always acknowledged," Mulassano specifies. "She would choose the photographer, she was the head of the visual bureau. They had lots of conflicts: neither Rosanna nor Giorgio has an easy personality. She was confident of her work, and he never told her she had done a perfect job. He treated her the same as he treated everyone else: at best, he would say you'd done a good job, and that was enough. Later, he would admit you had done something successful, never at the time. Never giving satisfaction to anyone, wrapped in a suit of armor. Because Giorgio's theory was that you should never say 'good job!' since that should be taken for granted, as a matter of course."

The year 1982 would be a milestone in Armani's history, even though it began with a certain amount of hubbub over the fact that the designer chose to show his womenswear collection, in March, to buyers only. Some believed that this new approach was prompted by Giorgio's irritation at the poor reception of the Japanese-inspired collection. Others thought it was nothing more than a way of standing out in a time of turmoil and clutter, a time when "everything was becoming an emblem of exaggeration, from the casting of models to the way that the press was brought into line," as Armani recalled. Whatever the reason, John Fairchild, publisher of *Women's Wear Daily*, who had long been one of Armani's major supporters, took it personally and swore vendetta. "Armani is trying to bridle the press," he stated. "We will stop covering his collection, and we won't mention the introduction of his new perfume. This business is difficult enough. If someone tries to go negative on me, to hell with him!" Armani replied that his decision had nothing to do with controlling fashion journalists but added, "I'm not interested in being judged by them either." Moreover, he felt that there was a gap between certain kinds of fashion and the real world: "Media coverage of a collection five months before it's in the stores is something that's more important to the fashion world than it is to the end consumer, which is who I'm working for."

The sting of Fairchild's boycott, which at first threatened to pose real problems, was soon soothed away by a wonderful surprise. Jay Cocks, now a respected motion picture screenwriter and at the time a film and music critic for *Time* magazine, had seen, in the late seventies—as he tells it—suits by an Italian designer in two exclusive shops run by friends of his, Alan Bilzerian in Boston and Max O'Blue in Los Angeles: "I noticed that a certain kind of customer was interested in those suits: younger people, often theater people, writers. Not the sort of people who are usually interested in fashion. I thought that they were incredible: you could wear that clothing and live in your own movie. They were imaginative, and yet at the same time they were very concrete, made with great discernment, with a rigorous professionality, and they were totally new. The shape was new and very relaxed, which was very important at the time. And so I started to buy them for myself." Cocks thought that it would be a good idea to go to Italy and write a story about this new designer. He suggested it to his boss, Martha Duffy, who responded enthusiastically. The editor in chief approved the idea without hesitation. And so, "one morning, the director of PR for Armani walked into the office and found a telegram on the desk announcing that journalists from *Time* would be arriving. The idea was completely ours," Cocks recalls.

> And all this became very important for Giorgio, because it was purely a matter of his talent. It wasn't about PR, no one was trying to sell anything. He really liked the fact that we were all fashion dilettantes; in fact, none of us were fashion journalists, none of us had ever written about fashion. And so we came into it with a totally

fresh approach. It was an enjoyable conversation—through an interpreter, because I spoke no Italian and he spoke no English. When I met him, I didn't know what we would say to each other, but it wasn't a problem. We talked about music, movies, food, and, of course, clothing, but in a general way. It wasn't the usual fashion interview—what colors we'll see this season, what lines next season, all those dull topics. Instead I asked him where he got his ideas, what he was trying to do with his fashion, what were his sources of inspiration. We talked about the movies we both liked, and we hit it off immediately. But I made sure, the first time I went to meet him, to wear an Armani jacket. I still have it. And so, as soon as he saw me, he understood that I was a fan, that I was there because I admired him. That's how it went, quite simply.

Time gave Armani the cover: a photograph by Bob Krieger and a headline that enshrined him in the pantheon of fame, "Giorgio's Gorgeous Style." Inside was an eight-page layout and a confident judgment: Armani is the best. The article by Jay Cocks began with a quote from an irritated Pierre Bergé, the partner and patron saint of Saint Laurent, who let slip an involuntary outburst: "Giorgio Armani! Except for white truffles, pasta, and opera, the Italians can't be credited with anything! Give me one piece of clothing, one fashion statement that Armani has made that has truly influenced the world." Cocks shut him down, listing the achievements of the Italian designer: "Alors, Pierre. The unstructured jacket. An easeful elegance without stricture. Tailoring of a kind thought possible only when done by hand. The layering of fabrics by pattern, texture, and color so that clothing takes on for a second the quiet shimmer of a seventeenth-century Japanese print. Surprising combinations of garments—leather pants as part of a suit, a long jacket over foreshortened slacks, a vest worn over a coat—that scramble clichés and conventions into a new and effortless redefinition of style. A functional celebration of fabric. A reshaping of traditional geometry with witty contours, sudden symmetries, and startling vectors. A new sort of freedom in clothes. An ease, the Armani ease. And that, as we say in French, is just for les openers."

Today, Jay Cocks still assures us of his total admiration for the Italian designer: "First of all, I often congratulate myself for having the brilliant idea of doing an article on Armani, because he continues to be a prodigious figure in the world of design. If you're in this business, what you try to do is to become increasingly creative, year after year. But at a certain point, you become a resident of Mount Olympus. Whatever you do, you're untouchable. You're above criticism. Because what you have done so clearly defines a personality and an era, that criticism can't affect you. There aren't many people who have reached that point: I guess Saint Laurent and Armani, and maybe Lagerfeld. I see Giorgio as a major resident of a large villa by the sea in this Mount Olympus."

Cocks enjoys telling about the diplomatic incident that was provoked by the *Time* article and the famous cover. Despite the fact that Armani and Galeotti had decided not to show their collections to the press that year, an exception was made for *Time*. "In order to do the article, we had to see the collection. And it was a special event: we were the only ones in the audience. Which, of course, made everyone else furious, including *WWD*. But they got over it after a few years; everything is fine now.

This was my first experience with the world of fashion, and with the levels of almost homicidal competition. But we had fun, the article was published, and this was roughly the period of *American Gigolo*, and so it was really a special time for him."

The article marked a point of arrival, a distinction dreamed of by one and all but achieved by very few. Since the end of World War Two, *Time* has given its cover to only a very few Italians: among them Alcide De Gasperi, Palmiro Togliatti, Enrico Berlinguer, Giulio Andreotti, Gianni Agnelli, Arturo Toscanini, Luciano Pavarotti, Sophia Loren, Gina Lollobrigida, and Bernardo Bertolucci—and all the popes, of course. Among the European fashion designers and couturiers, only Christian Dior, some thirty years before, had been celebrated for his new look. Even before Giorgio got the magazine in his hands, he ran into Valentino who, to his surprise, whispered in his ear the words, "My, my!"

"I didn't understand how important that *Time* cover would be. I was in Paris and I was walking out of the Ritz, when I saw my partner Sergio coming toward me, waving the magazine, with tears in his eyes. Sure, okay, it's just a magazine cover," Armani recalled in a video interview done in the same hotel, many years later, by Adriana Mulassano. But it was not just a magazine cover; it was much more important than that. It emphasized the seriousness of the company and Armani and Galeotti's commitment, and they both understood that now the real work would begin: "That cover made me suddenly feel the obligation of my position. We were almost obliged to begin retailing. Not only multibrand stores, but dedicated stores as well, in direct ownership, especially significant in terms of image. We became retailers on the fly, we had no experience." It was this investiture of responsibility, then, this sanctification, that most affected Armani's ego and revenues, which that year tripled, rising from 9 billion to 26 billion lire. Those who met Armani and Galeotti in that period were struck by the entirely new attitude the pair now had toward business.

A new era was beginning, however, with a new address: Armani and Galeotti moved their home and offices to Via Borgonuovo 21, in Milan. The palazzo had once belonged to Franco Marinotti (SNIA Viscosa) and the Riva cotton manufacturers; it was rented. The architect Giancarlo Ortelli cleaned the place up, stripping it of Pompeian panels, ornaments, stuccoes, and friezes of unknown origin, a process of reduction that reflected Giorgio's sober nature and his admirable honesty about his own origins. "The styles of the past have nothing to do with me, because I didn't grow up in venerable *palazzetti*, filled with history," he would say. "I've always lived in middle-class homes, because we weren't rich. I would feel like a liar and a little ridiculous if I invented an origin for myself that had never existed. Old objects have value if you inherit them, if your family has handed them down for centuries." In the spaces that once housed a sumptuous ballroom and a swimming pool, runway presentations would now be held. In fact, this building would house the most exclusive little theater on earth, cozy and private, featuring the now famous strip of light.

CHAPTER FIVE

Dark Years

Events, strategies, ideas, and awards of all sorts coursed one after the other in an inexorable torrent. In 1983 the Giorgio Armani Fashion Corporation was founded, again in partnership with GFT; the new corporation replaced the Giorgio Armani Men's Wear Corporation USA and took over all U.S. distribution. A boutique in Milan's Via Sant'Andrea also opened its doors. The city of Piacenza conferred a gold medal on Armani, and he received the Fil d'Or (Golden Thread Award) at the Festival du Lin (Linen Festival) in Paris, as well as the Council of Fashion Designers of America Award for best international fashion designer. It hadn't been that many years since Giorgio Armani had started his own label, but he was already astonishingly famous. "Rivers of words have been unleashed, words by Giorgio Armani, about Giorgio Armani, on behalf of Giorgio Armani, and against Giorgio Armani," wrote Adriana Mulassano in 1984. "Dozens of articles about his fashion philosophy, dozens of professional profiles, dozens of interviews, dozens of newspapers and magazines from around the world have written about him." Armani's official public image was being consolidated. His steady icy blue gaze fascinated fashion journalists, who compared it to that of a Siamese cat or a bird of prey, with this last attempting to draw comparisons between the acuity of his vision and the eyesight of the eagle that provided the image for his logo. A vast body of literature was devoted to the subject of his nose, and debates focused on whether plastic surgery had had a role in its perfection. Amid the deluge of coverage, a steady stream of aristocratic titles flowed his way. In the course of a decade, he rose from the rank of prince to the undisputed status of king. The moniker "King Giorgio" became a commonplace in fashion journalism.

Armani was as famous as a movie star, and praise was lavished on both his determination and the unwavering consistency between the aesthetic he proposed to the public and the way he lived his life. "A compact, modest, introverted image, neatly hemmed, timid, and a little thorny. Because what is especially surprising is that this is the exact same attitude that Armani presents to anyone he talks to: whether it is someone he is personally close to or someone he met five minutes ago. One has to wonder how it could be that, even though he is part of the star system, even though he lives under the constant glare of the spotlights, he never betrays a false note, he never lends his private life to the ravages of the gossip sheets." Many years ago, this is how Adriana Mulassano elaborated on her own rhetorical conundrum: "The same virtually mystical fanaticism that Armani lavished on his work, the same manic perfectionism that was such a crucial factor in his success as a fashion designer, the same remorseless sacrifices that form part of his fashion in imposing a style that is proof against the temptations of whimsy, all these elements are present in and central to his private life as well. It is pointless to ask him cunning or underhanded questions about his leisure time," she continued. "The answers are always the same: 'In the evenings I stay home. . . . I watch television . . . maybe with four or five friends. . . . I lead a quiet, routine life.'"

And it is remarkable to note that even today, when media culture is even more ferociously cannibalistic, all this still remains true. All that we know about him can be found in his professional profile. On rare occasions he allows himself a public observation, which the media do their best to transform into polemics, but mystery shrouds his private life. His life has a public aspect, and there is much reporting on dinners he attends or the celebrities who surround him, yet he often attends social events hosted by the powerful, the scions of the ruling class, or the most respected figures in high society and only a privileged few know about it. The latter activities belong to the sphere of his private life, and Giorgio Armani can afford to keep that private life private. This strict compartmentalization has always been one of his distinctive traits. Everyone remembers that Galeotti, from the very beginning, did everything he could to construct a network of protection around Armani, a defense mechanism, a filter between him and the rest of the world, to guard him against all unwelcome incursions. His extremely tight-lipped professional staff has also always done its best to safeguard this unassailable fortress of privacy—always loyal, always ready to form a human shield. Everyone defends him fiercely; everyone adores him and is ready to defend his hatred of criticism, saying, "Giorgio works in good faith, and so he becomes hypersensitive about his own creativity."

Armani has often described himself as a tyrant and admits that he can be very strict. He demands absolute loyalty, turning his back on anyone who leaves his orbit, yet his charm is nigh on irresistible. Working for Armani demands a particular set of character traits: patience, self-sacrifice, and a passion for fashion. "I know that I tend to centralize," Armani admits, "that I tend to resist delegating, that I trust only myself. People who think I'm tough on the job are right: I'm hard on mistakes, I don't allow room for error. I demand the best from others, but especially from myself; I'm never willing to settle, because there's always something better, you just have to try a little harder to attain it."

Armani needs a team, and his relationship with that team is always a dialectic, a creative exchange, and not always a peaceful one. "Provocation is necessary because it is stimulating, it triggers the ideas that slumber inside us, in the furor of our mutual hard edges. The loveliest things that we do are always done in the moments of maximum tension. If my closest colleagues on my creative staff are already good at what they do, in part it's because of our ferocious battles. By nature and by impulse toward discretion, I'm never overconsiderate. At the most, I might say with a smile, well, I really taught you well." Everything comes back to himself. Lack of modesty or fear of disappointment? Mistrust, delusions of grandeur, or well-developed sense of self-preservation? Whatever the motive that drives him, Armani walks a fine line between democracy and tyranny. He oversees every detail, even the flowers that adorn his gardens (in the garden in Milan, they must be pure white). He has a courteous word for everyone he meets, but his voice takes on the rumble of thunder if something seems even the slightest shade less than perfect, different from the way he imagines it. After the storm, his eyes regain their sky-blue color, filled with an azure light, and all is forgotten. And though Armani is stingy with compliments, rarely catering to the egos of those who work for him, the simple fact of his approval is received as a major achievement.

Armani's reserve stems from a choice he made a long time ago: work before all else, work as life. He himself admits that he decided to put work at the top of his list of priorities out of ambition: he wanted to be the first among firsts. Ultimately, this became the source of his passion, what allows him to experience unparalleled joy and excitement in his work. "There is nothing I love more than work, and in order to obtain this pleasure, I pay the price: first and foremost, a lack of liberty. Some people think that I am not very outgoing, antisocial, a bear, an ingrate, because in order to work I give up the chance to spend time with other people, and often that's a source of pain. How I wish that I could give to other people everything I'd like to give them; but the kind of work I do is tyrannical, it demands everything you have, it takes everything. It restricts your emotional range, because you know how little you can afford to offer, and so you feel that you cannot afford to take much either. The price that you pay is that in the end you are often alone: but you know that, you accept that." Thus Armani himself confirms it: there is another side to his heart, a freer side, open to adventure and surprise, a side only a very few people have seen (although in recent years he has finally allowed himself the luxury of admitting it exists, even indulging it to a certain degree). Those who know him well know that he is capable of great kindness, surprising acts of generosity. But he keeps a tight rein on his more frivolous impulses; for example, he loves all kinds of good food, but he has practically become a vegetarian. It is as though he were working constantly to repress part of his personality, as if to keep a promise he made to himself.

Giorgio Armani grew up in an atmosphere of discipline and self-sacrifice, and self-sacrifice became his way of life. That austerity has softened over time, keeping pace with a general quality of life that has improved exponentially, but we do know that the very first holidays he allowed himself were only twenty-five years ago, when he and Sergio Galeotti went to the Grenadines and he spent Christmas at Mustique. "That was one of his first real holiday trips. Otherwise, for a very long time, he spent lots of weekends at Santa Margherita, at my house," Rosanna Armani recalls, smiling as she thinks back to the long-ago summers when they would rent an inflatable dinghy in Greece. A recurring question Giorgio would ask his sister reveals the profound anxiety that continued to plague this man even after had become famous: "How much money do you need to be rich?" As if he dreamed of a threshold past which he could begin to relax.

Armani's self-abnegation was and remains proverbial. His own mother would often urge him to enjoy life more, as did Sergio Galeotti, his alter ego. Barbara Vitti recalls: "While Giorgio would gladly have stayed in the offices to work until midnight, Sergio, at seven in the evening—click, click—would turn off and then on the lights in the palazzo: 'Time to go home, everybody out of the building, please!' Giorgio imagined that everyone else's lives revolved around the Giorgio Armani company, but Sergio was generous in that aspect as well, in understanding that other people had other things to worry about, to think about, that they had lives of their own." Galeotti said again and again, when he saw his friend constantly so serious and so often gloomy, "Giorgio, you're young, rich, and handsome. What more do you want from life?"

We know that Galeotti played a substantial role in the growth of the Giorgio Armani company, yet he also knew how to foster a climate of relaxation and fun. He would make fun of Giorgio, accusing him of being a worrywart. Beppe Modenese remembers: "Once he lay on the floor and pretended to be dead, and Giorgio walked in and got really scared." Barbara Vitti recalls: "Sergio pretended to leave the house, but instead he hid under the bed. When Giorgio came back, he heard a spectral voice calling him: *Gioorgioo*!!" Another time, for Giorgio's fiftieth birthday, which happened to be on the same day as a runway presentation, Galeotti decided to organize a surprise party, with Vitti's help.

> We had handed out flashlights to all the guests, special flashlights that looked like little birthday cake candles. We had also ordered a huge cake—Doretta Palazzi had arranged the cake, and it had frosting that represented the facade of the palazzo in the Via Borgonuovo. At the time, I was in charge of the money for events and I hadn't asked for an estimate in advance. It was six in the evening: four delivery people arrived, carrying this immense tray with a cake on it. I looked at the bill, written out on a sheet of paper: 12 million lire [about $12,000 at the time]. I slumped over against the gate. I called Doretta, and she started to panic. In the meanwhile, everyone went down into the little theater, with their little cake candle flashlights in hand. They knew they were supposed to turn them on at the end of the runway presentation. We had paid for a blank full-page ad in the Corriere della Sera and in La Repubblica with a tiny headline, saying "Happy Birthday, Giorgio"; all of our manufacturers and suppliers had pitched in to pay for it. When Giorgio came onstage, at the end of the show, the lights went out, and you could hear him saying, "Shit, a power failure," and then suddenly,

unexpectedly, all the little birthday cake candles came on, and he started laughing hysterically. The cake was upstairs, in the garden. And I was worried sick about how much it had cost. Sergio had figured out that I was worried about something and asked me what was wrong. I said to him, "Have you seen the cake? How much do you think it must have cost?" He said: at least 13 or 14 million lire. And I said: no, just twelve. He figured there was no problem.

Because Galeotti had an open mind, he was a big-picture man, and he was ready to consider the most daring proposals—for instance, the enormous mural in the Via Broletto, which still sports huge images advertising Emporio Armani. Barbara Vitti came up with the idea of billboard advertising, but he took her idea and enthusiastically developed it, thus formulating a radically new approach to fashion advertising and communication. Very few people recall the debut of what has by now become just a another distinctive corner in the city of Milan: a photograph by Aldo Fallai depicting four relaxed young men dressed in deconstructed clothing and idly reading the newspaper. Subsequent images featured a variety of scenes—cityscapes, either very Milanese or exotic—with young couples. Often they were huge renditions of the covers of the magnificent magazine of Emporio Armani, founded in 1989, conceived by Giorgio and Sergio and edited by Rosanna Armani, a magazine that itself started a trend.

It was with Sergio Galeotti that Giorgio Armani began to indulge his love of houses. One of his dreams was to have a house in every city: "Everywhere I go, I'd like to own a house, rather than living in a hotel, because a house is a haven for me.

I have a pretty public life, and it keeps me very busy. When I come home, I want it to be in my own home, with the right atmosphere, a place where I can relax and have a sense of serenity." His Milan home, for instance, was conceived as a very bare space: "almost as if I hadn't moved in yet, where nothing is definitive or certain. I really love empty spaces, where I can always imagine adding things: I don't like the definitive setting, the finished thing, the handsome painting put in just the right spot, which means nothing else could be added there. That is why my walls are empty, unadorned."

The same principles are at work in his project, inaugurated in September 2000, to produce objects and furnishings for the home. They are a logical extension of everything we know about his style. While there are naysayers who consider Armani Casa to be of little importance, cold and impersonal, the close relationship between his idea of fashion and his vision of the home is clear: a sense of lightness, geometry, a certain discretion, along with a sense of total determination; a love of texture, of materials. Armani Casa is meant to give the consumer a sense of freedom, offering a totally clean and linear approach that verges on the obsessive yet leaves plenty of room for the imagination, for the event or performance that will be staged in the space it decorates. This respect for a physiologically disciplined aesthetic is very Armani. We can find evidence of it in his vacation photographs, which feature rows of distinctly diverse individuals, all of them the picture of sobriety, even in their summer relaxation and the simplicity of their wraparound skirts and Bermuda shorts. Armani cannot restrain his horror at vulgarity, his stylistic prudence, his all-encompassing need for calm, and this uncompromising aesthetic influences everything that surrounds him. "Giorgio," his sister says, "fixes things up everywhere he goes, adding things, as if he were dressing the set of a movie, to take possession of a place. It's as if he was driven by an old peasant impulse." Ironically, Giorgio has always envied Rosanna her love of travel and her total independence. "She is an artist working in holidays and leisure time," he likes to say about her.

In 1981 Armani had purchased six *dammusi*, or traditional cottages, at Cala Gadir, on the island of Pantelleria, a place he had discovered with Sergio Galeotti some time before that still casts a spell on him today. Restored by the architect Gabriella Giuntoli, they are surrounded by an extraordinary garden: palm trees, caper bushes, oleanders, cacti, orange groves, and olive trees and, amid the scents of lavender and rosemary, a magnificent swimming pool. The villagelike compound of houses has grown over the years, and it has been photographed countless times. It is here Giorgio goes to recover the sense of freedom he more often sacrifices to his work. The memories of his longtime friends all communicate a consistent picture of true happiness in Pantelleria. Adriana, Anna, Carla, Cristina, Natalia, and Rachele, along with his family and his closest and most loyal colleagues: they have all been present at that intimate time of the year when Giorgio finally feels free to express the lighter side of his soul, the part he normally keeps under tight control. "Pantelleria is a haven for me, an island that I first discovered many years ago, through friends of mine, and I immediately fell in love with this place because it remains, I believe, unique. There is nowhere like it on earth. It has a savage harshness, but also a gentle Mediterranean sweetness. When I arrive here, I feel totally open to anything. I am happy to go on outings, go to the beach, or stay at home, I become a human being again and I forget the demands of the rest of the year. I rediscover the simpler feelings. I am a little naive here." This is how he describes his house: "The interior is very spare, I didn't want to create a villa, it's not palatial: the colors are very subtle, there is almost never white, for instance, which is a strong, violent color. It's all shades of gray and *sabbia* [Italian for sand, used to denote a range of cream colors]."

A relaxed, perfect setting: "Each guest lived in their own *dammuso*. In the morning, everyone would emerge, dressed in a white linen robe," Cristina Brigidini, often a guest here in the seventies and eighties, remembers. "Then we would sit around reading newspapers. Then, without planning it out, we would gather again dressed in white or navy blue. They were fun, simple holidays, we were all young. Giorgio had lots of scooters, all identical, and we'd set off, like a swarm of bees, with bandanas wrapped around our heads. He was the first to use a Provençal style bandana. He had a huge white inflatable rubber dinghy, before he bought his sailboat. In the afternoon, we'd have mint tea, and in the evening we'd all go out to dinner in some little restaurant. Giorgio was always courteous and hospitable on Pantelleria. We would talk about fashion, sometimes, but not about his work."

Over the course of the years he has maintained the habit of gathering his own little tribe in the rocky and aromatic setting of Pantelleria. The colors of the rooms may change over time, but the spirit of the place remains intact, while the giant desalination plant turns seawater into freshwater, keeping the banana trees and palm trees flourishing.

Another place welcomes and protects Armani's most private moments. It is close to Piacenza, in Broni. He was looking for a *cascina* (an Italian country farmhouse), and even though, as always, what he had in mind was simple and unpretentious, he wound up agreeing to buy something far different in order to make Sergio happy: Galeotti, who was as curious as could be, had peered through the bars of an iron gate and discovered Villa Rivara, an aristocratic pinkish *palazzotto*, or mansion, with a marble staircase and neoclassical statues on the grounds. Almost as a game, he insisted on asking about it: "The house was for sale," Armani recalls. "It was in a state of neglect and was surrounded by a huge park, overgrown and abandoned, with lots of crumbling statues. A week later, I owned it. I immediately planned to strip it of its pompous decor and its pretentious qualities as a villa in which to receive and entertain. I wanted to turn it into a house that was comfortable and easygoing." Though it was not at all what Armani had imagined he wanted, he was to shape it into one of his most beloved homes, guided by his overwhelming aesthetic and as usual loyal to the principles of understatement, modesty, respect for his personal history, and above all the common sense that governs everything he does. "In the end, it became exactly what I wanted: I can have a considerable number of guests, and so it protects my need for privacy and my love of socializing and company." The architect Giancarlo Ortelli was hired to do the renovations, and it was the first house where Giorgio decided to forgo his usual beiges and other neutral tones. "It was a country villa, with chintz and other decorations. He kept the magnificent bathrooms, the staircase, the lake with swans. One white swan, and one black swan," Cristina Brigidini recalls with amusement. The black swan once chased her across the huge yard, to the amusement of Giorgio and Sergio.

The house in Broni, purchased in 1982, is in the eighteenth-century style, with columns at the front. The pomegranate-colored walls are lined with leather-bound treatises on botany.

The French doors overlook the little man-made lake and the well-groomed lawn, dotted with does and goats and dogs from the local pound. In short, it is impressive. And perhaps a little embarrassing—at least at first—to its owner. In an interview that he gave to *Vanity Fair* in 2000, Armani felt compelled to explain away the purchase of this sumptuous mansion as purely pragmatic, pointing to the renovations made by the previous owner, a toothpaste manufacturer: "See, that's why I bought it: it already had everything when I bought it, running water, air-conditioning. See?" In keeping with a principle he considered sacrosanct, he has never wanted to be taken for one of those who try to foist off false family histories: among his rare qualities is a refusal to turn his back on his modest middle-class origins. He has never claimed to be aristocratic or a member of the ancient nobility, as so many of his colleagues have.

His mother was often a guest at Broni, with her little dog, and his closest friends tell about the incredible Christmas parties, the many weekends, the relaxed evenings spent watching movies, taking long afternoon walks, enjoying simple dinners, "because Giorgio only serves caviar and lobster on official occasions, when he cannot avoid it, to maintain his image." A working office was installed over the stables, and Giorgio would often have staff meetings there. People still remember a wonderful birthday party, when Giorgio turned sixty; they also remember how, at the beginning, it was especially nice because Armani wasn't so busy then, and stays at Broni were simple and relaxed, time spent with friends in a comfortable country house.

All the while, the company was growing. Armani was increasingly overwhelmed with responsibilities and gave up many of the pleasures in his life to devote himself to work.

His relationship with Sergio Galeotti, however, was an enduring comfort to him. It made up for all the experiences he was missing outside the universe of Armani. But fate was lying in ambush. Though he had already survived so many ordeals, one of the worst was in store. His friend, his partner, the most indispensable person in his life, his alter ego, was ill. Sergio Galeotti began to display the symptoms of a terrible disease, the one most feared.

Sergio was wasting away. Barbara Vitti, who was close to him till the end, recalls a macabre but touching moment: "He knew that he was going to die. We knew it too. He said something really nice to us, when he was sick: 'You know, if you have me embalmed and you put me in a glass case, I'll stick around, and that way I can see you.' " Giorgio remembered his pain during Sergio's stay in the hospital in Paris: "During the year that he was sick, I helped myself get by with prescription drugs, to help me stand the sound of Sergio's voice on the phone. His voice was so weak, the voice of an old person. It was almost impossible to take. I reached out for help." Only work could help him to forget. Giorgio had considered giving it up, but it seemed wrong. "If I give up this work, I thought to myself, all of Sergio's hopes and dreams, everything that he put into this company, would be lost. I couldn't give in to that weakness. I had to do what I could to survive. I don't know how I made it, but I did. And it was this, and Sergio, still, that gives me the strength to carry on now," said Armani in an especially heartfelt interview in *Vanity Fair* in 2000.

Memory is one way of conferring eternity on those who are no longer with us. It can be done with private thoughts and small rituals. Giorgio Armani always carries a picture of Sergio in his luggage when he travels, and his picture is always there on Giorgio's worktable or in his bedroom. In those pictures, Sergio is always smiling, strong, with the eternal cigarette between his fingers. In the house that he shared with Sergio in Forte dei Marmi, Giorgio continues to see him: "He's always there. He's always in my head. I can see him, walking down the steps, in the garden with his cigarette, talking to friends. And so I go there, because Sergio was there, but it's hard. Very hard."

Galeotti died in August 1985. When Cristina Brigidini learned of Sergio's death, she hurried to Forte dei Marmi to be with her friend Giorgio. "I remember hugging him, and him weeping despairingly," she recalls. "Even now, if I think about it, it breaks my heart." "He was one of the earliest victims. Rock Hudson had already died. We didn't know exactly what had killed him," Vitti remembers. No one was talking about AIDS back then, and the news was reported to the media by Barbara Vitti herself, in a press release stating that Galeotti had died of a heart attack. All the newspapers, out of discretion or friendship, stuck to this official version, except for *Il Messaggero*, which reported the true cause of death. Immediately after the Rome daily published the news, Giorgio Armani announced he would withdraw all his advertising from the publication, as if in a final attempt to protect this man he had loved so deeply.

Giorgio's suffering was immense. It struck him as intolerable, profoundly unjust, that his friend should have died. An unbreakable bond linked the two of them: they had crossed over the territories of passion and succeeded in building a friendship based on exchange and mutual support that helped each reinforce his own identity, precisely because of how different they were. The loss went beyond time, existed outside of time, leaving Giorgio in the grip of melancholy and bitter reflection. One day, talking about his feelings to Edgarda Ferri and explaining his solitary bent, he told her he knew others thought him harsh. Acknowledging that he tended to be tough on himself and relentless with others, he said: "There are people I would like to ask to forgive me. Forgive me for lacking the patience and generosity required to listen; the depth of heart needed to understand; the compassion to suffer together. One of those people is no longer with us, I'm talking about Galeotti; I remember him standing in a doorway, lost, bewildered, saying: 'I wanted to talk to you, but you never had time for me.' "

CHAPTER SIX

Another Identity

The end of a life at the young age of forty is always a tragic event, but even more so when the one who died was not only your life partner but also your protector and guide: "Sergio helped me to believe in my work, in my own drives," Giorgio often said, well aware that he had been allowed to cultivate his creative impulses undisturbed primarily because his helpmeet had spared him so many responsibilities by taking care of the commercial side of the company. Following Galeotti's death, the private and intimate sphere began to overlap uncomfortably with the public. There was a radical shift in equilibrium, and within the corporation people began to wonder how things would be able to continue. Some people expressed faith in Armani, while others expressed doubts about his entrepreneurial abilities. The atmosphere was uneasy in part because so many people had expectations they felt were not met. There were those who thought they were Galeotti's moral heirs, people who raised his specter whenever there were decisions to be made. Probably, their invocation of his memory was not meant maliciously, but it contributed to the general sense of uncertainty throughout the company. "It created an atmosphere of division," Rosanna Armani remembered. "While everybody thought of Giorgio as the silent creative one who needed to be left alone, the role that Galeotti had played, and his own personal nature, tended to nurture immensely expansive relationships with everyone involved. While Giorgio was and remains inner-directed, it was so much easier to love Sergio because he was so direct and straightforward and intense in his relations with everyone, even though he frightened some people with his exquisitely Tuscan impetuosity. While he was cheerful and playful, Giorgio was more serious and self-aware."

And so, along with the grief occasioned by the unexpected loss, there was another kind of distress. Armani was suddenly obliged to deal with an array of challenges for which he was ill prepared. "He was profoundly harmed by Sergio's death, which was horribly untimely in business terms as well," Adriana Mulassano recalled. As he himself explained in an interview with *Il Sole 24 Ore:* "Galeotti was lost to the company at a delicate juncture, just when it became necessary to adopt a different set of policies from those that were suited to a family-run business." Among the complicated variables, Mulassano recalled that,

> since they had been equal partners in the company, Giorgio asked Sergio's relatives if they wanted to continue to be involved as his partners. But any relationship with Giorgio without the involvement of Sergio would have proved to be very difficult, serving only to sharpen the pain of not having him there with them. And so it was, having received a clear refusal, it became necessary to dissolve the company. Perhaps, with extreme shortsightedness, they also doubted that Giorgio, alone, would be successful. And Giorgio was indeed forced to start over practically from nothing. And so he invented skills in a job that he really didn't know, the work of an

entrepreneur. He was good at it too, doubly good, and showed remarkable strength. And that is why I have such an overwhelming admiration for him."

Mulassano went on passionately: "I know how much it cost him to start up again, leaving aside his grief at the physical and spiritual absence of someone of the stature of Galeotti, to find the courage to say: 'I'll go on alone.' So, if Galeotti had been a genius in launching Armani, Armani was just as much of a genius." She added a bitter but equally sincere note: "Even if he created this success of his with his own hands, it resulted in his becoming mistrustful of everyone else, once he discovered just how good he was."

One's reactions to the facts of life, to the ordeals life imposes, show the stamp of one's character. To the surprise and admiration of all who worked alongside him, Armani revealed his alter ego, a second self that deep in his heart he knew existed but had never revealed in the past. Even though there was no shortage of volunteers hoping to take over Sergio's many responsibilities, Giorgio decided: "Sergio is gone, and I will take over his role. I will succeed in doing this." For a year, he studied the situation carefully in order to understand exactly how his company was organized, even in those areas where he had never intervened directly. The intelligent but somewhat befuddled young man, isolated at his drawing board, slightly inclined toward the hermit's life and uninterested in the preoccupations of marketers and lawyers, faded away completely, and Armani embraced the larger world, assuming the twofold role of creative force and entrepreneur. He did not hang back, he delegated none of his responsibilities, and he did not allow others to intimidate him; he dug deep into the store of knowledge and experience he and his partner had laid away together. And he astonished everyone by extending his creative talents to the strategic and financial sector. As if he were working at two separate desks, he managed to play opposing roles, contradicting himself in full good faith as he took up both sides of a question: "After Sergio's death, I found myself obliged to imagine a different nature within myself, and I was spontaneously obliged to learn how to talk with lawyers, to say one thing and think another. I experienced a sort of twofold personality: first of all, I am a creative force and second of all, I managed to enter into the spirit of the other role, the job of an entrepreneur who judged a collection from a commercial point of view. And I contradicted myself, in the sense that what I had loved as a fashion designer until the day before, with figures before me, I found that I would stop loving it," Armani explained, looking back a few years later. To some extent, he even enjoyed this game of musical chairs—remember his boyhood love for theater.

A great optimizer, Armani at one point observed: "Certainly, it leaves me less time for the creative part of my work, but I don't see this as particularly harmful. Considering the pace I have to work at and the productivity I need to maintain, I have simply become more concise, better organized. I can no longer concede myself time to be uncertain." For the Giorgio Armani company, these were years of dizzying growth. As Cristina Jucker wrote in 1986: "In 1985, sales volume for the products of the Giorgio Armani S.p.A. [the main company in the holding group] was more than 280 billion lire. This figure also includes everything that was produced by other companies on an Armani licensing basis and distributed in the market. Also last year, however, the revenue of the main company alone was

47 billion lire, with a 25 percent increase over 1984. The revenue of the Giorgio Armani S.p.A. consisted of royalties, [fees for] style consulting, and commissions on sales. Overall, there are about 150 employees in the group."

The demands of managing a company whose activities now extended well beyond the boundaries of Italy posed new strategic and structural challenges. "Only 50 percent of sales, in fact, have to do with Italy," Jucker went on in her article, "another 25 percent is limited to Europe (especially Germany) and other countries, while the final 25 percent concerns the nations of North America, especially the United States, considered by nearly all the Italian fashion designers to be one of the best customer bases." Armani decided to reorganize the group, and in the course of a year, as he himself recalled, he worked to "review the internal structures and reinforce the weak points." A new financial director, Giuseppe Volonteri, was appointed, as well as a new sales director, Giuseppe Brusone, for years the marketing manager at Valentino; in 1994 he would be named Armani's managing director.

The next step was to reevaluate the arrangements with the companies that produced under the Armani label. But the chief focus was on the development of the Emporio Armani sector, which by this point had moved far beyond jeans to include a wide range of other products—even cashmere overcoats. New stores were scheduled to open, including a new Paris store, in the Place Vendôme, and other retail outlets in Europe and the United States. The Giorgio Armani company came to enjoy an enviable financial situation, both transparent and straightforward: all the new investments were self-financing, so there was no need for partners or any other help; most important of all, there was no need to rely on banks.

It was the close relationship between fashion designers and industry that developed around the seventies that had allowed Italian fashion to evolve as it did, until it finally became one of the most important sectors in the Italian economy. The first and fundamental agreement for Giorgio Armani had been with the Gruppo Finanziario Tessile (GFT) of Turin, which now produced the Mani collection and a menswear line, both of which were highly successful in Europe and the United States. Another major collaboration was with SIM, Società Italiana Manufatti, in Sassuolo, near Modena, which produced jeans and basic fashion for the Emporio Armani line and was quoted, beginning in 1986, on the Milan Borsa. Both companies benefited from the arrangement, to the point that Armani, responding to a journalist who had commented on the enormous advantages his company had brought to the Modena-based textiles manufacturer, answered that certainly the alliance had been positive, "but perhaps we might say that SIM was quoted in the Borsa in part thanks to the Giorgio Armani company."

At this time, a major change in corporate policy appeared on the horizon. Giorgio Armani described it in an interview with *Mondo Economico* in 1989: "We began working as consultants in the seventies, creating collections for a number of different companies. But the decision to become entrepreneurs ourselves came about when we presented the first Armani collection. It was one thing," he went on,

> to work as designers for various companies, and it's quite another matter to work on something that will bear your name. This was the first phase. In that period, we made use of licensing agreements, inasmuch as we needed well-structured companies that enjoyed their

own distribution networks. In time, as our name became better known, new problems arose. Then the time came when the designer himself felt the need to intervene in the area of distribution, in order to do a better job of safeguarding his name and reputation. Distribution is a function of the product that one is bringing to market. And often in the past there have been disagreements between manufacturer and designer on the best way to present those products and distribute them. In other cases, the industrial partner was reluctant to become designer-dependent and chose not to base its entire operation on the work of a single fashion designer. And so, on the part of the manufacturer, the need developed to make way for other labels, creating within the corporation a small stable or team of fashion designers. Sometimes this teamwork has been productive; in other cases it met with resentment. And that is why, now, the possibility of a different relationship had become clearer: the fashion designer no longer wished to be nothing more than a licenser, instead he wished to explore in greater detail the problems of production and distribution, to a greater degree than his current role seemed to make possible.

This new policy was a natural development from the brilliant innovations of Sergio Galeotti, as Carlo Rivetti describes: "I believe that the great success of Giorgio Armani, nowadays, is still the product of the distribution and marketing strategies that Sergio created. Thirty years ago, Italy was a different country, but Sergio's ideas were far ahead of the curve. I can't say to what degree this was fully informed managerial expertise, but the fact remains that he understood the value of things far ahead of others. He was one of the first to eliminate the middleman in distribution, and he realized that in the chain of added value, a great proportion of the value was being handed over downstream to the retailers. He blazed a new path, and it was the right one." The next step would be to work directly on the mechanics of production. The first phase involved the acquisition of 20 percent of the capital of SIM in 1989. This would lay the groundwork for subsequent joint ventures with other companies and a direct entry into the shareholdings of the industrial manufacturing companies.

Balances and structures were changing. Rosanna and Silvana—the daughter of Giorgio's older brother, Sergio—although they were already working inside the company, assumed new roles, attempting to fill the emotional vacuum left by Galeotti. They would become new keystones for Giorgio. Rosanna became director of the press office, as well as working alongside Giorgio to develop communication and corporate image strategies—by no means an easy task, since, as we know, Armani never likes to delegate anything, even to people he trusts.

Among Rosanna's many talents is an innate knack for casting, and it was frequently up to her to discover and recruit all those young people with interesting faces who turned up in Emporio Armani runway presentations in the early years. This aptitude served her well in her new position. Advertising campaigns and billboards that carry the Armani name always have a certain cinematic air to them. Giorgio's love of the movies guided the idiom he chose to represent the spirit of his fashion. The product tends to appear only obliquely; the stronger emphasis is on atmosphere. The images resemble movie stills.

For the first television commercial for Emporio Armani, in 1986, he decided to ask Martin Scorsese to direct. For "a commercial that wouldn't be a commercial," in perfect agreement, neither Armani nor Scorsese wanted professional models or actors. And so it was that Scorsese, on an improvised set in the large frescoed rooms on the Via Durini, came to shoot a thirty-second-long piece of film in which a young man and a young woman sat on a bed exchanging a few words of spare and urgent dialogue. The scene communicated a subtle sense of tension: everything was suspended, as if in a delicate amorous prelude. The result was outstanding. In 1988 a second spot directed by Scorsese, for Armani perfume, would win the prestigious Media Key Award. Rosanna Armani described working with the great American director: "I did my best to help Martin to stay relaxed; he is an unusual sort of person. I remember he would just get obsessed with things, nobody could smoke, absolutely, and there were moments when he would have to be completely alone for ten minutes, and he would communicate these demands through his ex-wife, Barbara. So I would do my best to ensure that he was left alone: it was important to have Signor Scorsese shooting a commercial for Emporio Armani."

Silvana was now in charge of overseeing the production of underwear, women's jeans, the Armani Bambino line, and womenswear lines for Emporio Armani. She had joined the company just a few years before, having abandoned without any real regret her youthful dreams of becoming a model and a fashion editor. This is how she recalls her start in the styling office: "I developed, laboriously, a huge packet of sketches of swimsuits. Giorgio looked through them hurriedly, picked just five, and told me that I would have to do better. Then he kept on telling me that, but the number of sketches that he approved grew in number."

Another major figure who was quietly emerging in this new constellation was Leo Dell'Orco, who had been present from the start but grew very close to Armani during Galeotti's decline. Dell'Orco worked alongside Giorgio designing the Emporio Armani and the Giorgio Armani Uomo lines. According to Adriana Mulassano and Barbara Vitti, he is an intuitive and lively individual. The tenacity that comes with his Apulian roots, combined with a fertile intelligence, resulted in his winning a central place in Giorgio's affections and in the company. People also give Leo credit for having softened Armani's personality: he is a courteous, sweet-natured person, with a gift for diplomacy.

Because a considerable number of important employees left in the aftermath of Sergio's death, Cristina Brigidini recalls, "there was a radical change. Giorgio had a fight with Barbara Vitti [his longtime PR person], and among those who left the company were also Doretta Palazzi, who was in charge of communications, and Marisa Modiano Bulleghin, a delightful, exceedingly elegant woman, very capable, who had been Armani's most important assistant for many years." To those who spoke of a general rush for the exits, Armani responded: "What an exaggeration. Four people left. It's true that they had important jobs and replacing them was a delicate matter, and I believed that a network of loyalty and solidarity, understanding, and daily cooperation had been built up. So that we understood one another with a glance, in a flash. Half a word. I had this illusion, and it hurt me. And where can we put the blame? On impatience, on the situation that brought about misunderstandings and confusion. I reacted in grief to Sergio's illness. I became rigid, trying to make people believe that nothing had happened, that everything was functioning exactly as before. I didn't want to talk about things. I couldn't stand that it was the topic of conversation, of gossip. I hurled myself headfirst into my work."

Armani became increasingly intransigent, refusing to entertain any opposition to his decisions. "Perhaps there is a certain amount of myth about it," one of his manufacturers, the industrialist Fernando Ciai of ICAP in Perugia, said in 1986. "You can't waste his time. On the other hand, he is a man under enormous stress, it's tough being number one. And it's obvious that he's number one. I'm just getting back from New York and I can assure you that he is the top in America. On the other hand, he has a combative, harsh personality: they are both sides of the same coin. Could he be the same great Armani if he weren't so harsh?" His chief manufacturer, Marco Rivetti of GFT, also defended him: "Yes, I have heard that lots of people have fights with him. But I don't. I immediately get along with him because he knows that I tell him the truth. In my opinion, Giorgio becomes aggressive when he suspects he is being had. On the other hand, he is so good at what he does, and now he has discovered this new skill as a manager: I am talking about strategy, relationships with suppliers, I am talking about what Armani will be doing in twenty years."

In all this, Galeotti's influence was perpetually present. The runway presentations held in the aftermath of his death were charged with such emotional tension that, as Kal Ruttenstein, womenswear buyer for Bloomingdale's, put it, "it was like attending a wake." So many of the achievements derived from projects he had envisioned, such as the inauguration of the Paris boutique, the elaborate contract signed in 1987 with the

Itochu group, for the promotion of the Armani label in Japan, and the subsequent opening of three stores in Tokyo. In a sense, another dream of his was also realized in 1986, when Jacqueline Kennedy's sister, Lee Radziwill, whom Galeotti admired enormously, was given an official position in the company: she became the elegant and invaluable supervisor of special events.

There was no escape from Galeotti's memory. When Gabriella Forte moved from New York to Milan to be closer to Giorgio, she took over the apartment on the Via Borgonuovo; even though he had lived there for only a short period, people continued to refer to it as "Galeotti's office" long after she moved in. All this no doubt only made Giorgio Armani's job harder. Working could not give him complete respite from his grief, and the stress hardened him further. He became increasingly miserly with his compliments. Every morning, on arriving at work, Forte was greeted with the comment "You need a face-lift, you look massively exhausted." No one ever heard him say, at the end of a long working day: "You've done a good job." At the end of the extensive negotiations for the Itochu contract, Forte recalled, "Armani signed and left. If we had commented on it to him, at the very most he would have said, 'Well, why else are you here?' " In Giorgio Armani's idiosyncratic approach to compliments and courtesy, there was no place for celebrating achievements he considered the obvious and unexceptional result of hard work. His inborn striving toward perfection quite simply could not admit the possibility of other outcomes. "With him, you had to pass a test every day," Forte said, "you were always starting over, proving who you were." Even Rosanna agreed: "If you got something wrong, Giorgio would kill you." There was no forgiveness. "The closer you were to him, the more violent his reaction would be. For Giorgio, there was no difference whether you were his sister or his doorman."

In the meantime, each new collection was hailed by the critics, and Giorgio Armani was honored by a long series of prizes and awards, the most symbolically significant being the title of Grand'Ufficiale al Merito, an honor conferred on him by Francesco Cossiga, then president of the Italian republic. Production continued to expand and diversify, for example, with a new line of underwear. Journalists were talking about an Armani empire: two thousand multilabel retail outlets around the world, eighty Emporio Armani stores in Italy, and boutiques in cities such as Milan, Geneva, Brussels, and New York, with the combined revenues from womenswear, menswear, clothing for young people and children, perfumes, umbrellas, jeans, and scarves bringing in a total of 250 billion lire.

His name on any product became a certificate of elegance, a sign of distinction, a status symbol. Taking advantage of this cachet, Armani launched himself enthusiastically on various adventures. He designed the costumes for Maruschka Detmers in Marco Bellocchio's movie *Il diavolo in corpo* (*The Devil in the Flesh*) as well as wardrobes for Harvey Keitel, Stefania Sandrelli, and Trudie Styler in Giovanni Soldati's *La sposa americana* (*American Bride*). Pope John Paul II commissioned him to do a new cover for the Gospel that is used in cathedrals during pontifical celebrations. He also designed the uniforms for the Foggia soccer team as well as those for the Italian national soccer team for the 1986 World Cup, played in Mexico. And who could forget Notturno, the sophisticated and laconically styled telephone designed for Italtel Telematica, the company run by his close friend and customer Marisa Bellisario? It is an austere but sensual object, with a band of light running through it, a sort of miniaturized, stylized reproduction of his oft-imitated little theater, illuminated only by the bright strip of the catwalk.

The big, renovated Emporio Armani on the Via Durini continued to be a focal point in the city of Milan, and the popularity of his soft jackets, evocative of the cardigan, his baggy trousers, his grays and beiges, in short, everything that made up the powerful image of Armani, grew and attained depth: his style became more a way of thinking than of dressing. That purified, ascetic aesthetic humanized by proportion and volume led to the creation of a new social category, an extended sect of the faithful: those who recoiled at the gaudy colors, at the unsubtle seductiveness, characteristic of a new fashion trend that would prove to be enduring. The glossy pages of the fashion magazines, the television screens, and the catwalks all offered slits, curves, and exaggeratedly clingy materials. It was the time of Azzedine Alaïa, with his form-hugging outfits. But Armani stood firm: "I refuse to use the most facile and trite mechanisms: showing breasts, placing bows in certain locations, squeezing another." Instead of the showy sexy look, he preferred the mystery of evening wear from the twenties or the thirties. The press recorded a pungent comment: "I would really like to see how certain new little idols, such as Alaïa, will do over the long run." There are those who say that behind the austerity of his fashion, there is a lack of love for women and for the female body. But the reverse is true: Armani's severe but flattering styles are a recognition of their worth, a sign of respect.

A moment of decisive consecration arrived in 1987, in the form of not a prize but involvement in one of the most important films of the period. Armani designed the costumes for the main characters in Brian De Palma's film *The Untouchables*.

Sean Connery, Kevin Costner, Billy Drago, Andy Garcia, and Charles Martin Smith made up the extraordinary cast, and the perfection of the wardrobe contributed enormously to the energy of their portrayals. The clothes were the epitome of that particular Armani style that drew its inspiration from the thirties and forties, and they garnered the film an Oscar for best costumes.

In 1988 Armani received, among many other awards and honors, the Cristobal Balenciaga Prize, awarded in person by King Juan Carlos of Spain, as the finest international fashion designer. Shortly after that ceremony, he flew to Los Angeles, where, for the inauguration of his boutique on Rodeo Drive, a major reception, complete with a runway presentation, was being held at the L.A. Museum of Contemporary Art (MoCA). An operation worthy of Fitzcarraldo, it caused Armani a good deal of apprehension: "For him, everything that is foreign becomes traumatic," Gabriella Forte recalled. "Giorgio always needs to maintain control over everything, and this time, in the United States, he had to place his trust in someone else's organizational skills." Sixty trunks were shipped from Milan in order to reconstruct inside the museum the entire theater of the Via Borgonuovo. Catwalk, staircase, padded seats, lighting: with disconcerting effect, everything appeared exactly the same as the original several thousand miles and an ocean away, much to the astonishment of the three hundred illustrious guests invited by Lee Radziwill. There could have been more—high society and charity are a very familiar pairing in this city—but that would have meant the evening's entertainment would have been open to anyone with the price of admission, and Armani wanted the event to be an exclusive affair. He got his way by making a substantial donation to the museum, in the guise of rent. On the restricted guest list were the most powerful and fashionable names in Hollywood, among them Richard Gere, Bob Dylan, Anjelica Huston, Martin Scorsese, Merv Griffin, Eva Gabor, Amy Irving, and Steven Spielberg. It was a very Hollywood audience for an evening that ended with dinner and dancing. And it was a memorable society event, characterized by strong contrast: the flashy aesthetics of the Californian audience was in sharp distinction to the spare sobriety of the Armani style. "Personally, if I look at the clothing in the collection and the audience that watched the runway presentation, I see no relationship," Gabriella Forte commented the next day. "These things demand time, culture, and education, they take a while to evolve."

This would remain a significant moment in the history of Armani: it represented an important step forward in his relationship with Hollywood, which would go on consolidating until it became a routine interaction. Armani's collaboration with Gabriella Forte and Lee Radziwill was invaluable, but it was when he hired Wanda McDaniel, a writer who had covered the film industry for the Los Angeles *Herald Examiner*, that Armani invented a new way of communicating. McDaniel was married to Albert S. Ruddy, a well-known Hollywood producer, and counted many influential people among her friends. It was easy for her to persuade a number of stars to wear Armani suits during the most important events. Nowadays, this gimmick seems obvious, and in fact there is what amounts to a race among designers to dress people for the most prestigious testimonials, but in 1988 the idea of giving clothing free of charge to the best-known celebrities of the moment so that they would wear it in public on official occasions was a pioneering maneuver.

Giorgio Armani himself, while watching a video of De Palma's *Scarface* (1983), identified Michelle Pfeiffer as one of the actresses best suited to his fashion, so it was to Pfeiffer, not yet a top-ranked star, that McDaniel offered a contract. At the 1989 Oscars she wore a long dress and a jacket with silver buttons; not yet accustomed to the idea of borrowing expensive items from jewelers, she sported McDaniel's engagement ring. Her absolute elegance was immediately noted; *Women's Wear Daily* ran a headline reading "The Agony and the Ecstasy." Side by side, it mercilessly compared two photographs: the horrible satin outfit with a single sleeve worn by Kim Basinger—who had decided to try her hand at fashion design with her friend Prince—and the splendid sobriety of Michelle Pfeiffer dressed by Armani. Wanda McDaniel also got in touch with Jodie Foster, who had just been the target of a swarm of negative comments over the light blue taffeta gown with a huge bow in back that she had worn when she walked up to get her little gold statue as best actress for her role in Jonathan Kaplan's movie *The Accused* (1988). She suggested that the actress consider wearing Armani, and from that moment on he became Foster's favorite designer.

Just as French and Italian actors wore outfits by the most famous couturiers in the fifties and sixties, now all Hollywood began opting for clothing by Giorgio Armani. It was the beginning of a tradition: a great many stars from all around the world still wear Armani to official ceremonies. The criteria for being adopted were highly selective: the celebrities who wore Giorgio Armani clothing not only needed to possess characteristics that harmonized with his fashion, but they also inevitably wound up entering his orbit. The fashion designer established friendships with them; he would spoil them, organizing dinners, some official and some private, and often go so far as to share with them his rare moments of relaxation in his fantastic vacation homes.

The initial plan announced in 1986 that called for the opening of 150 Emporio Armani shops in the United States and 30 in Europe would be recalibrated, the focus shifting to the size of the spaces, rather than their number. Among other projects, a new Emporio Armani was opened in London: eleven thousand square feet and, on the third floor, the first Armani Caffè. Between buying a blazer and a jacket, shoppers could enjoy a pizza and a salad. The expansion strategy for Emporio Armani, which Armani called "my favorite creation," called for 10 new boutiques in England, 10 in Germany, 4 in France, and 75 in Japan. A large Emporio Armani opened in Manhattan in 1989.

In Florence, Armani decided to resurrect the historic restaurant Doney, which, from the early years of the twentieth century till its closing, had been a favorite of the beau monde and members of the international intelligentsia. It now faced an unexpected new fate: "I was looking for an unusual location for the Florence Emporio Armani. In the Piazza Strozzi, quite close to the famous Palazzo Strozzi, I noticed that the six large display windows of the Caffè Strozzi were shuttered: I took it over, and I discovered that the café had been given the Doney license. I remembered that quiet, refined, dignified restaurant, where I had spent a few enjoyable hours, and I decided to reinvent it."

Of the eighty-six hundred square feet of the new Emporio Armani, fifteen hundred were set aside for little culinary delights. The architect Giancarlo Ortelli imagined two separate entrances, one for the shop and the other for the restaurant. Armani for once abandoned his usual minimalism, selecting antique wooden furnishings and insisting that the setting mimic the warmth of times gone by. He hoped opening the restaurant would reassure those who were concerned about the invasion of boutiques in a city that many could hardly recognize anymore: "I really don't even expect to make money on it. I truly want to give back to Florence an easygoing space with a select, refined, exclusive quality, where there could be exhibits of fine art books, for example."

But Florence didn't measure up to Armani's expectations: "Two years later," he recalled in a 2002 interview, "with considerable bitterness, I was forced to shut it down, which made room for the adjoining Emporio Armani. The adventure cost me quite a lot of money, but it gave me a useful lesson for later enterprise." The experiment may have proved to be one of his few unsuccessful undertakings, but it is eloquent testimony to Armani's nostalgia for a certain cultural atmosphere, for a world that no longer exists.

The eighties were an intense decade for Giorgio Armani, marked by tragedy but also by great achievement. He had learned to take on the challenge of working with an increasingly frenzied and cynical market, and he had conquered the world. By now rich and famous, he chose to remain independent, and, turning down a chance to become the creative director of Lanvin, he instead kept on taking personal risks, putting himself into play rather than simply enjoying his success. In 1989 he justified his hyperactivity to Giusi Ferrè: "There is a logical, obvious reason, which was not under my control, and which I am forced to take into account. There are only the narrowest margins for maneuver, markets open and close rapidly. No one can sit and wait for an opportunity. Look at the case of my underwear collection. It came out in February 1986, it was very successful, with excellent prices, and honest quality.

At that point, Benetton announced triumphantly: Hello, I'm doing the same thing! How can you react? By researching, imagining, and designing new things." From serving as a distraction from his grief, work became a necessity for him: "At this point in my life, nothing could be more important. I could no longer take it, nowadays, to be unsuccessful. Every time, I do my best to make it a little further along, and that effort absorbs nearly all of my energy."

In this period when public and private events came thick and fast, Giorgio Armani felt more than ever before the need to define and consolidate the little tribe within which he felt truly safe and protected. With his sister, his niece Silvana, his friend Leo, and his closest friends, he goes on the short holidays he permits himself in August and at Christmas. This is when he finally achieves the modicum of carefree enjoyment of which he is capable. Particularly memorable was the time he spent in Africa, in 1989, when he finally achieved an old dream: being "on a farm, lost in the distance, impossible to track down, in the Africa of the vast spaces." Here is how his friend Emanuela Testori remembered the adventure:

> We went to Kenya, one Christmas, expecting to go on the usual safari, and so we weren't sure what to expect. We imagined the usual tourist experience, some tremendously kitsch thing. Instead, it was one of the nicest trips I've ever taken. We had terrible luck, it was supposed to be beautiful weather, it was the right season, but instead it was just raining and raining. Giorgio hadn't wanted to take a plane from Nairobi to Masai Mara, because he was worried about the weather, so we started off by jeep. The tracks were washed out, they were just rushing streams,

jeeps were getting bogged down; the lodge where we were heading was totally flooded so we wound up having to go to another. Everything was kind of make-do, certainly not a rich person's vacation. . . . And he had a wonderful time, it bothered him least of all of us. Giorgio is fantastic, he behaved like a child, he would push the jeep when it got stuck in the mud, he would laugh . . . he has an adventurous spirit and an extraordinary ability to adapt to situations. A man like him could be spoiled, but instead he adapts to any situation and never complains.

CHAPTER SEVEN

Staying Faithful

Eight years had passed since Armani had appeared on the cover of *Time*, and the USA that was governed by George H. W. Bush devoted an entire week of recognition and awards to Armani, in November 1990. A major article on the front page of the *Wall Street Journal* described him as "the conqueror of Manhattan." New York's Fashion Institute of Technology presented a spectacular exhibit of two hundred photographs: "Images of Man," curated by Richard Martin and Harold Koda, told the story of the revolution that Armani brought about in men's fashion, beginning with his deconstructed jackets as far back as the midseventies. Marshall Blonsky, a professor of semiotics, devoted a chapter to Armani in his book *American Mythologies*. "The case of Armani is an oddity," Blonsky told the *New York Times Magazine*. "He is not an intellectual, but he likes to play with ideas."

One memorable evening was the gala event at New York's Museum of Modern Art, featuring the American premiere of *Made in Milan*, the Scorsese film about Armani's work. The America that matters was in attendance, from politicians to cultural leaders and, of course, the entire world of film: from Robert De Niro, Isabella Rossellini, and Richard Gere to Cindy Crawford, Sigourney Weaver, and Matt Dillon. That night, the film was hailed as a great success (at the world premiere, at the

Venice Film Festival in September, it had met with a lukewarm reception), although some accused Armani of megalomania, of having erected a monument to himself. He responded: "Not at all. It's a medium-length film made for specific commercial purposes. My American division—and people should keep in mind that we have turnover in the United States of two hundred million dollars—wanted some footage on the way I work. At that point, we thought: we could turn this into a movie. That's what they're asking for in Japan, too. . . . We could give it to the fashion schools."

Made in Milan was a half-hour movie made by a world-class crew: Martin Scorsese directed, Nestor Almendros shot, and Jay Cocks wrote the screenplay. This is how Cocks describes the relationship between the Italian designer and the great director: "Seeing Martin and Giorgio together is an amazing experience. They are both people who usually do things their own way, and each has a system of his own, but the results are always fantastic. With two such creative individuals you can have a marvelous collaboration, or it might turn out that they just don't talk to each other. In this case, the result was fantastic. It was a movie about creativity, about the shared creativity of Giorgio and Martin. It was a fascinating way to do a movie about a designer, a way of exploring Giorgio's technique, but also Martin's technique, whether in the movie, the clothing, or the city of Milan, which became the costar of the film." Still, Giorgio said that he wasn't fully satisfied with the result, though his respect for Scorsese remained profound:

> I think that he could have done more if we had had an opportunity to talk in an unhurried manner. I don't know, it just seemed like we never talked. We had so

little time, just five days to shoot the whole thing. It was July, and everyone was tired, dangerously tired; I felt helpless to make things work. I had a major director and a script written by an important screenwriter. But I wasn't happy with a number of points. Some of those were eliminated, but a great many stayed in. I knew that we were dealing with a really difficult subject. Either they could show Armani in a dreamlike situation, or else in the harsh reality of our everyday routine. They could put the accent on Armani, who is still an attractive man with light blue eyes. Or else show him exhausted and worn out. There were a thousand different paths we could have taken. I'm not clear which path we took.

This was the very tenor of the criticisms leveled at the movie in Venice.

The film received a lot of coverage. "Unfortunately, I prefer to have just a few articles, but positive ones," Armani said. Talking about his work, "very simple, with an everyday routine, no real emotional drama," he said that by the beginning of the nineties he already felt as if he were swimming against the stream: "I'm a revolutionary, and I'm unwilling to accept the way the system works. I am fed up with overemphasis, contrivance, and insincere enthusiasms." In a period when fashion designers were being treated as divas, Armani said:

> It's . . . an environment that I really don't like anymore, for an array of factors that, on the one hand, delight me and, on the other hand, disappoint me profoundly. During the real boom time, people who made slippers were suddenly creative forces. Dressmakers promoted

themselves to fashion designers. The entrepreneur who manufactured fabrics launched himself into the luxury business. Suddenly everything was permitted, everything was possible. Certain sectors of the press, on a quest for something to cover and sources of advertising, were constantly standing ready to hail the new miracle, the new wonder. And every time that happened, there was another degree of escalation: c'mon, pour it on. Leading to an endless series of excessive imagery and nonexistent market. Until we arrived at this Place Pigalle puppet theater that stands before us now.

When one interviewer asked him whether he had a personal bone to pick with Paris, which at that point was generating an exuberant, perhaps even excessive style of fashion, he replied: "Well, that depends. I am certainly irritated by noise, by the circus atmosphere. The desire to astonish, whatever the cost, to leave the audience openmouthed, even if you have to fan bare breasts and codpieces in their faces—the French are masters of that line of entertainment, though the Italians rival them, admittedly. Ever since people decided that the ultimate purpose of every collection is to break the rules, all sorts of things have been happening." And he certainly didn't pull his punches:

> I only insist on pointing out that what is happening hasn't been the work of a single season. It has been the product of a chain reaction. To start with, in order to provoke a reaction and get attention, people started exaggerating with the color of a normal jacket. Then they added some weird accessory, say a stoplight hat or a brooch shaped like a fork. Then they needed more. To get people

to talk about that blessed woman's suit, they had to come up with something else. So they needed to eliminate a sleeve and cut in the back all the way to the belt. Next thing you know, there are feathers on the derriere, and the audience watching the show applauds and laughs. But these are just simple tricks designed to attract the public's attention. At this point, it strikes me that the reaction that's been simmering inside me is a reasonable one. It forms part of my creative baggage, and it grows with each magazine cover, each television special.

Armani began to wonder whether there was any reason to continue showing his collections with runway presentations. It wasn't the first time he'd felt this way: in March 1982, following the Japanese collection, Armani realized that he had indulged the trade press too much and, in agreement with Galeotti, decided to "withdraw from the scramble." Always clear-eyed about the world around him, he responded to the general *grande bouffe* of fashion with a yearning to restore things to their proper proportions: "What are fashion designers, after all? A group of ladies and gentlemen who design clothing. But that's not enough, people want more, it fails to stimulate the imagination. And so people start to mix up strange brews: culture, art, spiritualism. Or else they emphasize the society angle, or they position designers as mentors of lifestyle and gracious living. And I disagree with that. So let me say: I want to be clear about this. I make clothing, and that is how I want to speak to people. And if I manage to connect with a general trend of some sort, or if I am a bellwether of a deeper movement, that's fine. But my message remains: this jacket, that skirt, or this pair of trousers."

Fashion had worn out its welcome, it had become overexposed, and, more than weariness with this or that item of clothing, there was a dangerous phenomenon: people began to ignore the authority of fashion designers. "It's true. I perceive a sense of irony, a general rejection, people saying: Who do they think they are? What do they want? It's the product of that exasperation I was describing, that wretched excess. The mass media decided to transform us into superstars, good at everything. And we are good at what we do, in our sector. But in other fields, in other areas, they shouldn't even be asking our opinion."

It is true that an overenthusiastic press had attempted to transform this relatively new category of skilled artisans into spiritual gurus, qualified to opine on existential topics of all sorts. Whereas in the sixties, the important figures in society had been poets and photographers, in the eighties fashion was one of the most popular and significant fields all over the world. Giorgio Armani, unusual in his awareness of his own limitations as well as those of others, refused to be canonized: "I'm just a human being. I work from eight in the morning until nine at night. I don't have much time available to read and learn. I don't believe that I can create an opinion by asking my PR people to tell me about shows and send me catalogs." Armani's words seem prophetic: "I am baffled by these overarching ambitions, which would demand a very different life from the one a designer normally leads. As far as I am concerned, I have no specific objectives, I appreciate the simplicity of an ordinary life. I truly enjoy the pleasure of modesty." And by modesty he meant a healthy sense of self-criticism and a limited urge to be in the public eye. "Say little. Show off as little as possible," are his wise recommendations. "Avoid television, the gala in honor of such-and-such, or the drawing room with so-and-so . . . even though the circular success that demands almost nothing—just showing up—is very tempting. If you are lucky enough to come out with a short, intelligent observation, if you appear likable, if you don't look any older or fatter than the way the spectators remember you from last time, then it works fine. Get one thing wrong, and in five minutes you've undone years of work."

The euphoria of the eighties had finally come to an end. A major transformation that was under way would lead to conditions that could not have been foreseen even a short while before. The fall of the Berlin Wall, in 1989, took on a symbolic significance: not only did it mark the end of the cold war, but it represented a watershed that would have an impact on the rest of the world. Two strong factors were affecting Italy. The first was the crisis of the traditional political forces that had dominated the stage for so many years, even though they had long shown increasing signs of weakness. The major parties were experiencing a serious crisis of identity, and this made room for new political formations. The leagues [regional protest movements] blamed the national malaise on the Roman power center. The more highly developed north, with its wealth and industry, was at the heart of the conflict, objecting to the tax burden and adopting a confused populist platform of ethnic exclusion. At a time when talk was turning to globalization, the ideas being expressed in northern Italy were basically secessionist. Yet this was merely a faint echo of what was happening just a few hundred miles away, in the former Yugoslavia, where a bloody ethnic war raged. Between 1990 and 1991, the world also witnessed the first war in the Persian Gulf, the result of the unexpected invasion of Kuwait by Iraq under Saddam Hussein.

The institutional crisis in Italy was increasingly serious. Political and administrative scandals followed one another in quick succession, and, to make things even more complex, there was also the problem of the Mafia. The year 1992 was terrible in this regard: in March the Christian Democrat parliamentarian Salvo Lima, considered a major linchpin in the relations between politicians and Mafiosi, was gunned down; in May the magistrate Giovanni Falcone, a leading figure in the battle against the Mafia, was also assassinated; and in July a bomb killed Judge Paolo Borsellino, a close friend and colleague of the late Falcone in the *pool antimafia* of the Italian district attorney's office in Palermo.

The second major factor in the transformation that would mark the nineties was the Italian magistrature's battle against political and administrative corruption, which involved and in a sense indicted the country's entire governing class. Words like *bribe* and *Bribesville* became part of the common parlance, ultimately linked to the names of politicians, financiers, and even a great many representatives of Milan fashion, among them Armani. The expression "Clean Hands," the name of the judicial investigation, characterizes the entire era, a great swirl of confusion that, amid accusations of illicit party financing, corruption, and much more, culminated in the prosecution of the high and mighty, with news of their arrests and trials crowding the front pages of the nation.

In the meanwhile, the close-knit structure of the Italian textile manufacturing system was falling apart. Giorgio Armani, in an article that appeared in *Mondo Economico* in 1990, stated, among other things: "If we are talking about Italian Style in the physical sense, in terms of manufacturing, the difficulties and the risks of a system of production that is entirely located in Italy are potentially quite serious. And that is why we must do everything we can to modify our manufacturing structures.

Those structures have become sluggish, with a false sense of safety generated by the idea that successful design could endlessly take up the slack for their inefficiency." Later, in 1992, Marco Rivetti, chairman and managing director of GFT, said, in the context of a lengthy debate over the now-official crisis into which the sector had slid: "The underlying problem is being competitive. In a product such as menswear, where the labor content in the manufacturing process may be three hours of work, the cost of that work is a decisive variable. In China or in Romania, we can produce at a tenth or a twentieth of the cost. There are a series of companies in various countries to whom we have sold our know-how. Aside from Italy, we also manufacture in Spain, Germany, Austria, Hungary, the United States, Mexico, and China. In China, one hundred miles outside of Beijing, we have started an experimental project, a joint venture that is already producing 200,000 items a year, but that will soon double in capacity." So what would become of the labor force of the textile industry in Italy? Rivetti answered: "It's too soon to say. But European forecasts tell us that in fact textile manufacturing will disappear in western Europe, and that we will lose 300,000 jobs. In Italy, manufacturing niches will remain, nothing more." In short, everything was changing, and changing radically—in the country, in the mind-set, in the lifestyles, and, of course, in the perceptions of fashion.

Fashion designers adhere to a seasonal calendar, which inevitably means their vision of the world is frequently characterized by speed and shortsightedness. Only a very few designers had the foresight to understand that fashion was on a slippery slope, that owning status symbols was no longer enough for consumers. The very figure of the fashion designer had been so overexposed that its luster was beginning to fade:

people already had plenty of clothes in their closets. "It was an expected drop, at least in Italy," Marco Rivetti commented, "where people have always spent 8 percent of their income on clothing, as compared with an OECD average of 6 percent. But things are slow everywhere: in England, in France. And in the United States, there is an even more distinct phenomenon in declining spending on luxury apparel, and consumers are reducing their spending even further. A fundamental change." In 1991 the increase in imports (up 35 percent from 1990) was sharply inferior to the increase in exports (up 1.8 percent, mostly in the knitwear sector), resulting in a drop in the trade balance of more than 10 trillion lire (roughly $10 billion). GFT closed that same fiscal year with a loss, the first one in its sixty-two years in business.

The ostentation and bombast that had marked the previous decade were already losing force when Romeo Gigli arrived on the scene at the end of the eighties. He had been the first to offer a precious, exquisite fashion, a new intimacy, having sensed the new needs of the consuming public. The Japanese designers—Yohji Yamamoto, Issey Miyake, Rei Kawakubo—had already debuted in Paris with collections that would establish the vocabulary of fashion for the years that followed. From the very first runway presentations, it was clear that they would be changing the direction of fashion. Expiation was in the air, and the Prada phenomenon found fertile soil in the general desire for mortification. Gigli had already eliminated padded shoulders, but he had done so while introducing an exotic, romantic element; now, instead, an openly punitive aesthetic was on the rise, and it would ultimately lead to a revolution of the ugly and the unpleasant. Silhouettes were shrinking, shoulders were drooping, models no longer smiled, and photographers' success was determined by the degree of existential malaise they managed to express. Opulence and excess had inexorably devolved into a dim sensibility that resembled boredom and wallowed in the deathly hues of decadence, shuttling the public straight into the realm of cynicism, which was the other face, the productive face, of nihilism. Piercing, tattooing, and scarification became common practices, the only realms of independence available. The production of pain became the sole antidote to the ostentation of superficial prosperity in which one and all had participated with such blithe frivolity.

In fashion, the mistake was finally legitimized, recognized as a human trait, in an attempt to restore realism to everything that just a short while before was being treated in an overblown and triumphalistic manner. After years of marching to the ruthless rhythm of "Material Girl," sung by a then-plump Madonna, diametrically opposed emotions would now find expression in the ascent of the British art avant-garde, with the provocations of the Chapman brothers, the organic musings of Damien Hirst, and the legitimation of such desperate individuals as Orlan, who transformed art galleries into sites of disease through his pitiless documentation of operations performed on his own body. All those who had been giddily dining on champagne and oysters until the day before seemed to have found a new enthusiasm for the smell of hospital rooms. What had once been ignored or dismissed as uncomfortable or out of place was now trendy. In Italy, only Nanni Moretti and Giorgio Armani remained true to their worldviews. Each of them, in his own way, was steadfast in his loyalty to the language that he respected and that distinguished him. Moretti, in the guise of a character in one of his movies, slapped a fashion journalist for using the wrong word, while Armani, with his elegant and universal style that had survived intact over the decades, seemed unshakable, refusing to be swept up in the trends, ignoring the small or large shifts of the seasons.

Armani would, however, be obliged to weather aesthetic hailstorms, torrential downpours of chaotic ideas. Eventually the Belgian avant-garde and the pupils of the Saint Martin's School of London would rush unchecked onto the international stage and the glossy pages of the magazines, but already in the second half of the eighties Armani found himself defending his understated colors against the tidal wave of French exuberance, led by Christian Lacroix, who had electrified fashion journalists with his voluminous, encrusted, and fringed baroque outfits. But Armani's great and official antagonist was Gianni Versace, with his acrylic hues, his punk references, his byzantine bombast, and the vast spectacular stage mechanism that thrust sexuality and excess front and center, provocatively introducing all of it in the higher-toned drawing rooms. All this, of course, was the opposite of what Giorgio Armani loved and continued to love. In an interview with *L'Espresso* in the summer of 1992, he indulged in a bit of invective, though never naming names, clearly aimed at none other than Versace, bemoaning the portrayal of women as "mere attractions for men, vulgar sexual fantasies incarnate, nightclubs where stripteases are staged for the provincial wolves."

While the trade press was writing that whips and a sadomasochistic look à la Allen Jones were the latest thing, Armani's runway presentations favored natural colors, soft skirts, kimono-sleeve jackets, and straw hats. Armani sailed elegantly through the fashionista storms, remaining faithful to himself and his own beliefs. Certainly, he needed to make some modifications: trim the silhouette, shorten the jackets, and narrow the shoulders, but generally he would continue to offer a timeless fashion, respected and familiar. He stayed true to his own stylistic and conceptual identity, if indulging in a few extra colors and occasionally giving in to a print, like the Polynesian prints for the summer of 1993 or the Matisse-inspired prints the following winter. "All of my work is based on those very neutral tones, in part because they were very anonymous," Armani explained, while admitting that his mother's criticism of one of his more homogeneous collections—"Giorgio, all these beiges, maybe you should forget about them"—was not entirely off the mark: "My mother panned the collection, and she was right that time."

More than ever before, the strategy at the Armani Group was directed toward consolidation. Certainly, turnover was not overlooked, but more than increasing turnover, the focus was now on fine-tuning the group's corporate image. No other fashion designer, in fact, with the possible exception of Ralph Lauren, was so determined to identify and articulate the profile of a specific way of life. The success of Giorgio Armani's career was based on the principle of loyalty. Armani, working with the same stubborn determination he had shown since he was very young, was pursuing a goal: his ambition was to build and convey a universe of signs that express him, that represent him. In the world of Armani, clothing transmitted sensuality, but without sexual overtones. The clothing was a foreshadowing, an allusion, but never an explicit representation of physicality; that remained a private matter. His colors were soft. They subtly illustrated sensations; they never created them. His legendary shades of beige, which include all the chromatic hues of *sabbia*, Italian for a creamy white, served as a backdrop for potential bursts of color. And his real talent lay in the sphere of modulation, in the way he was able to respect an unwritten yet clearly established set of boundaries, stopping just short of them: raspberry, not shocking pink; mango, not orange. There was always a margin for the imagination.

Fashion is fickle by its very nature, and in the nineties fashion victims found themselves chasing after new idols created and celebrated by the trade press. Armani seemed to be falling out of style, but in reality he was opening stores all over the world and becoming increasingly popular. In 1991 he received an honorary degree from the Royal College of Art of London, in a magnificent ceremony at the Royal Albert Hall. The stars of Hollywood continued to wear Armani, and not only for Oscar night (in 1992 the ceremony was dubbed the "Armani Awards" by the press): Annette Bening, Anjelica Huston, Kevin Costner, Jodie Foster, and Tom Hanks are just a few of the celebrities who have worn Armani in a movie or in real life. He constantly outsold all other European fashion designers. Even Eric Clapton, who wore Gianni Versace on his 1990 tour, converted to Armani because he preferred the fit and the flow of his styles. Versace was so offended that he compared the singer-songwriter's new image to that of an accountant.

Skirmishes over the relative merits of the two designers swept the small but prickly world of fashion. Fashion journalism coined unwieldy adjectives such as "Armanian" and "Versacian" and used them whenever possible. The vendetta culminated with a face-off: the world literally had to choose between the runway presentations of Armani and Versace. To the astonishment of both the Italian and the international press, both had chosen the same time and day: 7:30 P.M. on Tuesday, September 8. Neither was willing to back down. Finally, following the interventions of Rosanna Armani and Santo Versace, an amicable solution was found—much to the relief of Beppe

Modenese, the Gran Cerimoniere della Camera della Moda (Master of Ceremonies of the Chamber of Fashion). Italian fashion has always suffered from personal feuds, so much so that even today it is difficult to consider it a monolithic organism, and many thought that the whole feud had been a publicity stunt, but nevertheless the rivalry between these two designers split the world of fashion into two armed camps.

The challenge facing Giorgio Armani was how to maintain control over every detail even as his company spanned the globe and comprised a vertiginous array of marketing and organizational details. It was an enormous task to preserve the stylistic consistency of the products he was selling around the world. The location of each button or the logo on a simple T-shirt was the result of his express wish. His obsessive need to control the environment and modify it to suit his own image was limitless, extending even to the uniforms of the waiters and staff in the Caffè Armani in Milan and London or the presentation of the chocolates served with the espresso at Doney, his restaurant in Florence. Wherever it took place—Los Angeles, Tokyo, Paris, London—every one of his runway presentations began with the delivery of a vast arsenal of supplies that included everything required to reconstruct exactly the relaxed and tranquil atmosphere of the Via Borgonuovo in Milan (from the jackets for the waiters, to the tablecloths and the beige or aqua upholstery for the chairs). He paid attention to the distance between the clothes hooks on the racks in his stores, wherever in the world they were.

Once again, he had a famous director, this time David Lynch, direct a commercial for him: "Chi è Giò?" meaning "Who is Giò?" referencing a nickname for Giorgio. Shot in black and white, the ad covered the full range of emotions, arrayed with a carefree sense of fun, intended to portray the effect of his new women's scent, Giò. The party held in the summer of 1992 for the debut of the perfume was subjected to the usual relentless directorial control. "A small crowd has gathered at the gate of the Armani estate at Broni, outside of Milan," read an article in the *Times Saturday Review* on August 8, 1992, "peering into the windows of each Mercedes that speeds through the entrance. The light of candles trembles alongside the drive leading into the park. On the right is the hunting lodge where Armani greets his guests. On the left, a stone staircase leads to the terrace where dinner will be served. Here, the activity is frenzied." Among the two hundred lucky guests were Eric Clapton, Lauren Bacall, Martin Scorsese, Christopher Lambert, Ornella Muti, and Lindsey Owen-Jones, the CEO of L'Oréal, which would be marketing Giò. Nothing was left to chance. Armani personally oversaw the seating chart, making last-minute changes, assisted patiently by his hyperefficient staff. Amid the candles and the place markers, the centerpiece featured the ingredients of his new scent: roses, orange blossoms, tuberose, and vanilla bark.

Another spectacular party was held in New York in February 1993. Sheldon Solow, owner of the Solow Building, a glass-clad skyscraper, offered the use of the building's immense basement and loaned for the event a charcoal drawing from Matisse's Moroccan period. Armani again directed the evening in detail, re-creating the rarefied atmosphere of an oriental dream. The setting was an orange grove illuminated with lamps imported from Tangier, furnished with low tables and immense, custom-manufactured sofas, above them ceilings of airy gauze. The menu offered couscous and caviar, delivered to the guests by waiters dressed all in white, while Moroccan musicians and belly dancers provided the entertainment. The international beau monde attended: Eunice Kennedy, the sister of the late John and Robert, with her husband, Sargent Shriver, and her son Bobby; Tama Janowitz, author of *Slaves of New York*; Robert De Niro, Dustin Hoffman, Martin Scorsese, Spike Lee, Sigourney Weaver, Linda Evangelista, and many others. The dinner followed the runway presentation of the summer collection, once again in a theater identical to the one in Milan. The collection was greeted with enthusiastic applause, and it was just as spicy and exotic as the meal that followed. Armani had negotiated a path through the various cultures of the Middle East and North Africa, fetching up on the beaches of Tahiti: soft jackets with a manly cut worn over striped silk pajamas; an interplay of proportions and combinations, contrasting materials and designs, for smock frocks over tapered pants; fairy-tale fabrics for the evening wear; elementary shapes, often reminiscent of the sarong, covered with sumptuous embroideries. It was an artistic exploration, a multicultural hymn, at a time when age-honored principles were being called into question and an insidious intolerance was in the air. The Israeli writer Amos Oz had been awarded the 1992 Frankfurt Peace Prize, and Armani, if only through his clothing, was showing that the fusion of cultures, symbols, and meanings could produce nothing but cultural and social harmony.

Events followed at a breakneck clip. In 1992 the Le Collezioni line for spring-summer 1993 was shown at New York's newly renovated Solomon R. Guggenheim Museum, where a Dan Flavin retrospective show was on view. In June of that year, Armani was invited to represent Italian fashion in Florence, at Palazzo Pitti. It was a celebration of the fortieth anniversary of the prêt-à-porter shows, with an exhibition at the Sala Bianca, an installation designed by Gae Aulenti. It was in that very space that Italy had launched its challenge to French fashion, through the work of the visionary impresario Giovanni Battista Giorgini, who had seen the potential of Italian style before anyone else. The naysayers had a field day, because Armani had not participated in the original Florentine debut, even though now his name was one of the most famous symbols of the triumph of Italian fashion around the world. Only a small number of his legendary blazers were exhibited; Armani preferred to show a series of evening gowns he had designed between 1982 and 1992, the better to underscore a personal victory: the press had dared to say that evening gowns weren't one of his strengths, and he had proved them all wrong. He had arrived late to the field of evening wear, the reason being the attendant financial demands: "You really had to invest, and we weren't ready to do it. So when we decided we could afford this step, I had to face the challenge that it presented to me and my style, in competition with some of the finest designers around. I tried to use surprising fabrics, lace, and embroideries. I played with light and shadow, and if I look at my creations, one after the other, they strike me as spectacular. But with the reassurance, the comfort that comes with the offer of a single image, the same idea of women."

The goal of remaining faithful to his identity was a recurring theme, but Armani also loved to amaze and contradict himself, to react. Fashion was going through a very complicated moment, and Giorgio Armani decided this would be a good time to shake things up, to wake Milan from its slumber. He carried out his plan in March 1992, during Milan's fashion week, with a big party at a well-known local disco, the Rolling Stone. "Dress as you wish!!!" were the words that appeared on the all-black invitation (no doubt Armani was responsible for the triple exclamation marks). It was a party in spectacular style. The huge hall was scented with roses—he had air-freighted eighteen thousand from Marrakesh, Morocco—the café tables were covered with red tablecloths, and the intimate lighting helped to create a bewildering atmosphere. The show was a cabaret featuring the queen of nightclubs, from New York's Copacabana, Susanne Bartsch, along with her troupe of transvestites. A huge crowd of young people, unknowns, and journalists packed into the crowded space, alongside Tina Turner and Seal, Kim Basinger and Barbara Rudnik, Robert Wilson and Nobel Laureate Camilo José Cela, as well as many important figures from the world of finance. Armani amused his guests, but he also nailed home a clear message: he was at the height of his success, with a sales volume of close to 800 billion lire (about $800 million), a consolidated group turnover of some 400 billion lire (about $400 million), and profits of 60 billion lire (about $60 million). He didn't throw the party just for fun or to further his image but because, as he said afterward, "It's a very serious way of making sure that I don't take myself too seriously."

The party also announced a subtle but important change of direction. The dawning of a new era had already been heralded in 1991 with the opening of the first A/X Armani Exchange store in SoHo, in New York. There would be forty more, and they would sell affordable jeans and T-shirts, manufactured in Italy by Simint (the former SIM), a company quoted on the Italian stock exchange and now controlled by Armani together with Finarte, owned by the Milanese financier Francesco Micheli. The new approach, which featured a domesticated, casual Armani style—naturally, of the finest quality—was a success. The public was tired of the slick, and designers were turning to the street for inspiration; this shift to what came to be dubbed street style did not catch Armani napping. He had an unquestioned instinct for picking up on social changes that would soon translate into aesthetic and consumer trends. He had proven with the inauguration of Emporio Armani at the beginning of the eighties that he knew how to hear and respond to the demands of mass consumption. And now, again, he was already ahead of the times.

He had always based his fashion on freedom, expressing ease through an entirely personal use of volumes and fabrics. Over time, many designers had adopted his aesthetic, to the point of excess in some cases. All the world was suddenly vibrating to the sound of a chaotic and nihilistic music that was extremely popular among the young. Grunge (from *grubby* and *dingy*) had developed as a reaction to the clean and conservative rock of the eighties. Two postpunk groups, Sonic Youth and the Butthole Surfers, tired of the traditional standards of health, beauty, and ambition, had already adopted a diseased, homeless, purposeless image. But the group Nirvana launched the style that created an aesthetic that corresponded to the music: organic, muddy, sticky. For a few pessimistic observers, grunge spelled the death of prêt-à-porter, but this is what Armani had to say: "If grunge means everything that is dirty, shabby, and cheap, then we must admit that this 'trend' is more fashionista than any other fashion. If, on the other hand, we use the term to describe the freedom to wear whatever we like, blending the individual items in a new and unaccustomed manner, then I embrace it wholeheartedly: in fact I have been purveying my style for the past eight years as the greatest possible level of freedom."

A new generation of aggressive and iconoclastic designers was emerging in the field of fashion. The old aristocracy of

Italian style was now being crushed between the demand for big numbers and a general inability to create anything new. Between the economic difficulties and the stylistic problems, it looked like the industry was adrift. The authoritative American trade magazine *W* attacked the phenomenon in a 1993 article that recognized Armani and Versace as the representatives of the establishment of Italian fashion. "Sure, we need new people," Armani said, "people who know how to work without the frenzy of thinking about turnover and nothing else, people who can blaze the path for new aesthetic and sociological trends. I can't do it because by now—as everybody says—I am part of the establishment, and I am obviously somewhat conditioned by my own credibility, by the need to sell my own clothing, by the structured clientele that I have won for myself. So let's make way for the young people. Though let me say this loud and clear: I haven't noticed any young designers that strike me as particularly interesting." Armani claimed that the "new angry stylists" were too detached from reality: "They tend toward an absolutely unjustified excess of creativity, a very limited sensibility for everything that appears wearable and comfortable. In other words, they fail to understand that futurism and visionary work may be exciting in terms of the creative ego, but they have no right to citizenship in the world we work in. And as if that weren't enough," he went on, "there is also the problem of conquering territory: because we, that is, myself, Gianni Versace, Karl Lagerfeld, Ferrè, and Valentino, have already taken over a great many of the niches that are available. And there isn't a lot of space left."

Armani was busier and busier. In 1993 he finally bought a house in Saint-Tropez, realizing an old dream he had shared with Sergio Galeotti. In 1971, during one of their many short trips to the Côte d'Azur, they had fallen in love with the region and thought about buying some land, but at the time they lacked the resources even to try. Now, Giorgio could afford it. With the help of his sister, Rosanna, and a few friends, who arranged appointments with a local realtor, he went to see three houses and bought one of them that same evening. He chose the house that had a human dimension, not the impressive show mansion. It was what Armani called "a true country house, you can hear the sound of the sea, but you can't see it, there is a swimming pool and seven palm trees." He renovated the house in a single week, keeping it in the Provençal style. It has the faded colors and spare beauty of a beloved home. And it is probably the house that most resembles his inner climate. The residents of Saint-Tropez like to talk about his appearances in town, absolutely anonymous, riding his ordinary bicycle.

Yet this was the same Armani who loomed so large on the international stage. He continued to receive awards and honors: an honorary induction into the Brera Academy, the Golden Effie Award for the ad campaign for Armani Jeans in the United States, the Aguja de Oro Award, the Telva Triunfador Award as the best fashion designer of the year. In 1993 he hosted the popular NBC television show *Saturday Night Live*. In October 1994 President Bill Clinton conferred on him a Lifetime Achievement Award. This important career recognition is bestowed by the National Italian American Foundation (NIAF) on the most respected Italians; Valentino is the only other designer to have received one, in 1989.

In December, in Los Angeles, on the occasion of the annual Fire and Ice Ball—to raise funds to fight women's cancer on behalf of the University of California—Armani presented his spring 1995 collection, in the immense space of Twentieth

Century Fox's Studio 15. This was his second runway presentation in Los Angeles. But something had changed since his first, that affair at the Museum of Contemporary Art in 1988 where the style of the guests was so at odds with their host's. Hollywood was dressing more soberly, with more restraint, perhaps in part thanks to Giorgio Armani. "It is comforting for me to see that in the context of a world that is usually so emphatic, women's fashion is becoming more understated," Armani said with respect to the event. "I remember that at MoCA, six years ago, I was horrified. I wondered how my fashion could win favor with women who wore certain outfits: lovely, but so very different from my style! Today, I see a great many more people seem to be adopting the Armani style."

In March of that same year a survey done by the *Financial Times* among fashion professionals crowned Armani "king of fashion designers," the most successful on earth, in terms of both sales and influence on the world of fashion. Everyone loved him, and everyone wanted to know how he inspired such devotion. Among the many possible answers, one seemed to predominate: Armani used communications and publicity to impose his aesthetic. He understood better and faster than others that every means of expression should be used to communicate one's interpretation of fashion, which, in his case, corresponds perfectly with his way of living in the world: sober but incisive, surprising in its consistency but also simply surprising, in a way that made him the talk of the town—and the planet. The presentation in October 1994 of his summer 1995 collection, for example, captured the attention of the press with what was clearly a great revolution in the House of Armani: the designs included short skirts, corsets, and skimpy tops—all things that were new for him, an exploration of another way of being feminine, a form that involved sexual rhetoric and stiletto heels.

He continued his now-intense collaboration with the movies: his clothing was worn by such actors as Lena Olin and Richard Gere in Mike Figgis's movie *Mr. Jones*, Roberto Benigni and Claudia Cardinale in Blake Edwards's *Son of the Pink Panther*. Lauren Bacall wore Armani in Robert Altman's *Prêt-à-Porter (Ready to Wear)*, as did Uma Thurman and Ving Rhames in Quentin Tarantino's *Pulp Fiction*. Even the wardrobe of the cast of *Così fan tutte*, in Jonathan Miller's production at the Royal Opera House in London, wore Emporio Armani. In 1994, for the sixtieth anniversary of the birth of Donald Duck (Paperino in Italian), Armani designed an outfit for him: a double-breasted suit, of vaguely grunge inspiration, a Nehru shirt, and a brightly colored jacket.

Armani, too, turned sixty in 1994. For the occasion, at the end of his menswear show in June all the models came out onto the runway—to a standing ovation—wearing black T-shirts bearing the Roman numerals for the numbers 60 and 20: Armani's age and the age of his career as a designer. That evening, there was a huge Indian buffet for 260 guests in his apartment and the garden in the Via Borgonuovo, specially decorated to evoke an oriental atmosphere: white linen wall coverings and, in the garden, tiny cages with red- and amber-colored candles lighting the warm evening. There was no becandled cake, however: Armani celebrated his actual birthday in Broni, on July 11, with his mother, his sister, Rosanna, his nieces and nephews, and the rest of his clan. Without spectacle and ostentation, as is his way.

New stores opened in Dubai, Seoul, and Singapore, but 1994 would be one of Giorgio Armani's most difficult years. First, there were serious financial troubles brewing at Simint. Armani had become an investor in the company in 1989 with a 20 percent share, and in 1994 he took it over altogether: "We realized that there was a worrisome series of management and organizational inefficiencies. We pointed that out, trusting in the fact that matters would be settled, and instead things moved in a different direction." Finarte sold its share to Giorgio and Rosanna Armani and to the Singapore businessman Ong Beng Seng, previously Armani's partner in a number of retail businesses. "A few months later, in April, we realized that there was 180 billion lire [about $180 million] missing, and no one had said a thing." The costs of Simint's investments in the United States had badly undermined the group's profits. The debt load proved to be overwhelming, despite the enormous success of the A/X Armani Exchange retail chain, and so—despite Armani's efforts to preserve the jobs at Simint—in order to protect the interests of small shareholders, Armani was obliged to sell the inventory, the licenses, the existing stores, and the name of the American operation of Simint USA to the Ong group. It was a major failure for Giorgio Armani, who was accustomed to winning, and it reinforced his belief that he could rely only on himself.

On top of this, that same year he ended his invaluable working relationship with Gabriella Forte, who had been his precious right arm, his closest colleague for fifteen years. Forte left to take a job with Calvin Klein, Armani's toughest American adversary. Lee Radziwill, who had been his special events organizer, also left. Worse: the most important names in Milanese fashion found themselves involved in very unpleasant problems with the law. The Italian magistrature was interested in investigating him as well. Indeed, the nationally renowned judge Antonio Di Pietro, chief investigator at the time, said to Armani, after inviting him to come in to his office for a conversation," I asked you to come first of all, because we know you are the most important designer." "Di Pietro is much more elegant than you might think from television," Armani quipped later. "And then, that toga Italian judges wear doesn't do much for him, especially when he wears it over that red vest. In person, he is actually much more elegant." Leaving aside the wisecracks and the playful tone he tried to project in a number of interviews during this period, the truth is that for him, as for many other Italian designers who were dragged into the investigation, it all came as a jarring shock: "The second great shock of my life, after the death of my partner, Sergio Galeotti," he later admitted. His career had always been marked by transparency and absolute honesty, and during this ordeal he continued to show great fortitude and a total good faith. In the end he emerged untouched by the scandal, having faced the questions and insinuations with a sort of fierce innocence—much, it seems, as he had responded to attempts to solicit bribes: "When I was asked to comply with a certain request [for a bribe], I was told that it was a normal practice, customary. I had never had anything to do with this sort of thing. I was kind of horrified. I asked if there were problems: they told me that it was just a way of speeding matters up. There were some administrative logjams for our company."

Throughout the investigation, he never neglected his professional commitments. He would answer the magistrates and the journalists who were persecuting him and then go back to fine-tuning the hem of a cocktail outfit or resume the fitting for an impending runway presentation. All around him, on the runway and on the rows of seats in his little theater, there was the usual tightly controlled chaos: dozens of shoes, belts, bags, scarves, hats, necklaces, items of jewelry, shawls, glasses, swatches of cloth, and stockings. With the mastery and authority of a conductor leading an orchestra, Armani would guide his colleagues, who would obey his every command, giving shape to his master plan. Bitter and a little hurt, he nonetheless worked on, determined. Once upon a time, he had never had to deal with these practicalities, back in the days when, as he himself has said, "Sergio protected me from everything. For me, the outside world was a foreign country. I had a special exemption to be a fashion designer." Over the years, however, he had been forced to learn a great deal and to become accustomed to handling all manner of everyday details. Where once, like a monarch, Armani would never handle cash, which he entrusted to his bodyguards (though in part this was due to his legendary obsession with hygiene), at the beginning of the nineties, Gabriella Forte tells us, she was amazed to see him pull a credit card out of his wallet and pay the check at a restaurant: "Giorgio is growing up; he is very proud of his credit cards and I have noticed that now, when he leaves Italy, he carries his own passport."

CHAPTER EIGHT

Conquering the World

"Sadly, I've lost contact a little. This is terrible because I want to live in the real world," Giorgio Armani admitted to Eric Clapton in a long and fascinating interview that was published in *GQ* in October 1995. "Whenever I can, I escape from my bodyguards. But the last time I took a bus it cost 50 lire. There was a driver and a ticket guy. Now there is only one person." Armani lives in a narrow, circumscribed world, surrounded by a lot of people, by his family and his closest colleagues, and even though there are times when he would like to be alone, in reality he is afraid of solitude. He's afraid of himself, of interacting with himself. He admits there isn't much about himself that he likes and that he would like to be a great many things that he is not: taller, less shy. More of a man of learning—and he utters a statement that, in reverse, is reminiscent of a Borgesian anxiety: "I'd like to be many things I'm not. I want to be a man of culture. To have read a lot of books. I have hundreds of books in all my homes, but it's difficult for me to imagine myself reading a book because it seems to me that first I would have to read everything that has been written before being able to read the latest books."

He says a great deal in that unusual interview, which ended up more of an honest conversation between friends: he talks about his awareness of his great influence but also says he always has a goal before his eyes and emulates the models that inspire him (his first sources of inspiration were the Duke of Windsor, Fred Astaire, and the actors in American movies). He says he loves seeing men cooking: "You know in the American films when you see men in the kitchen chopping onions . . . I love that!" He goes on to say that he finds himself in an odd situation, in which he is constantly thinking of the new and therefore surrounds himself with young people, often forgetting entirely to socialize with people his own age. He doesn't seem like a very happy person (the Italian commentator Giorgio Bocca called him "the Unhappy Prince" in his 1993 book *Metropolis*), though he admits that he remembers nothing important from the dark period of his life, when Sergio Galeotti fell ill and died. He feels that he erased all that in self-defense, but he knows the pain is always lying in ambush. He also confessed to Clapton that he once tried cocaine with a group of friends. Just once. He liked it, but that was the end. And once he tried acid, and all he could remember was a terrible pain in his kidneys. He says that he doesn't know how to smoke anything and that he thinks of all this dabbling in drugs as an experience to go through—obviously, without getting trapped in it. He is perfectly aware that in the world of fashion, it is said that a great many people use drugs, but he insists that this doesn't happen around him, adding, with a hint of irony: "I don't understand but when they come here maybe they feel like they're in church." He shares many reminiscences—among them, that as a child Tarzan was his hero—and notes with amusement that he had stopped driving about ten years before because he is excessively fond of speed. He talks about the cars he has owned: a Triumph, then a Porsche Carrera convertible coupe, and a Mercedes coupe. About his love of Ferraris, but the fact that he thinks it is too much trouble to own one. But to me his most important revelation is this: "I always want to remain like me, and even more, the more important I become, the more I like being me, with my defects, my insecurities. This is how it seems to me: the more a man remains himself, the more admirable he is."

He always dresses simply, in dark blue. His wardrobe now fills up an entire long hallway, and there are forty-eight separate doors to his closet. His house in the Via Borgonuovo occupies two stories: fifty-four hundred square feet of peace and quiet, basic shapes, and neutral colors—ivory, ecru, off white—with a few points of black for emphasis. All very thirties. Palm wood, parchment, oak. There are about fifteen rooms, overlooking an inner courtyard and a private garden. Five cats move freely among bronze statues of bears, panthers, and jaguars. Armani has a cook, a valet, a dresser, and two concierges. Lots and lots of paintings, but none of them hanging on the walls, which must remain uncluttered and creamy, like so many horizons. There are boxes everywhere, made of all sorts of materials from everywhere imaginable: "I saw a book of work by Jean-Michel Frank. I absolutely had to have a home like that. I wanted boxes to put things in. I wanted a container home. In the Frank style." A Chinese carpet in the huge dining room, with its parchment-paneled walls. And, of course, orchids in every corner: "I grow them in my house at Broni, in the Pavese region. When they bloom, I bring them to Milan." The luminous veranda on the top floor is where he stores the gifts he has received: among them, a large photograph of Andy Warhol and Liza Minnelli; a portrait that Michelle Pfeiffer gave him as a present; a metal jacket, the gift of an English sculptor; model cars from the thirties. In all this, you can sense the hand of Peter Marino, the Italian American architect who also decorated the

Agnelli family's New York home and who has worked with Armani on many other projects.

Armani perfume bottles are on display in the sumptuous bathroom, including Acqua di Giò, the most recent arrival, which received the Telva Triunfador de Belleza Prize, one of the many awards he received in 1995, along with the Together for Peace Foundation Cultural Award and the Maschera d'Oro Prize, to name just two. *Marie Claire* UK named him fashion designer of the year. Armani was working more and more in the world of film, in a wide variety of styles. His designs were seen on Enrica Antonioni, John Malkovich, and Sophie Marceau in *Beyond the Clouds*, the film by Michelangelo Antonioni and Wim Wenders; on Nicole Garcia and Marie Trintignant in *Une Fille Galante*, by Nadine Trintignant; and more major actors besides than there is room here to name. On April 7, 1995, in the context of the larger exposition "Kino, Movie, Cinema," celebrating the centennial of cinema, at the Martin-Gropius-Bau in Berlin, an exhibition opened with the title: "Armani vis-à-vis Dietrich." Even those with no special interest in fashion considered it an interesting juxtaposition. Time was compressed, and the dialogue between the restored clothing of Marlene Dietrich and the designs of Giorgio Armani was startling: the archetype of an elegance that rejected ostentation, an androgynous style that never turned into mere cross-dressing. Marlene loved tuxedos, men's overcoats, tailored jackets, loose trousers, and embroidered fabrics for long, flowing evening gowns. All this coincides perfectly with Armani's style. There is a remarkable correspondence, apparently derived from a shared sensibility, from a common interpretation of such concepts as femininity, space, and practicality, an urgent need to narrow the boundaries between the masculine and the feminine found, especially in

Armani's early work. All of it is protected by imperatives that guided and guide them both: class and confidence. For the event, Peter Lindbergh shot a series of remarkable black-and-white photographs. In part thanks to Armani's clothing of Armani and skillful makeup, the German photographer worked magic: the magnetic and ambiguous gaze of Marlene Dietrich seemed to come back to life in the eyes of a young model from Arizona, Amber Valletta.

After the runway presentation for the gala benefit held in Studio 15 at Twentieth Century Fox in Los Angeles, Giorgio Armani was an enthusiastic fan of huge spaces and the air of festival that hovered over that American adventure. He decided to attempt something similar in Milan. He had already fallen in love with "that sort of beautiful cathedral that is the Ansaldo," a huge factory, no longer in use, on the southern outskirts of Milan, and it inspired him to rent from the city government Padiglione 36, a huge industrial shed, for three seasons of runway presentations. The alluring location "had to be adapted to our needs"—at a cost of 50 million lire, with a further expense of 180 million lire later on. Ultimately, amid a bustling bazaar of limousines and media stars, from Claudia Cardinale and Ornella Muti to Isabelle Huppert and Eros Ramazzotti, fashion journalists from all over the world witnessed a spectacular runway presentation. Armani had imagined it as "a movie studio, set up as if we were making a major fashion movie, not like the recent Altman film *Prêt-à-porter (Ready to Wear)*, but perhaps more similar to Irving Cummings's *Vogues of 1938*, with the most famous models of the period wearing the name of the product they were advertising, such as Miss Lux Soap or Miss Pepsodent. Or else the Italian film *La contessa di Parma (The Duchess of Parma)*, directed by Alessandro Blasetti, with Elisa

Cegani and Maria Denis. Both of those movies date from 1937, which was roughly the year that I wanted to evoke with this installation." The 37,500 square feet of the pavilion were carpeted in black wall to wall; sixty-five models would present the clothing in a large hall set up with a 157-foot-long catwalk. On the walls were projected silhouettes of vintage lamps, while lanky Californian palm trees were visible through the tall windows. The dinner for twelve hundred guests was served on tables covered with black tablecloths. A staircase led up to a full-fledged nightclub with a black mosaic bar, black tables, and red lamps. The effect was spectacular and bewildering. It was a Thursday, March 9, and, at the end of the evening's entertainment, the doors were opened, and the city entered the space Armani had transformed into something entirely foreign. Young men and women, many coincidentally clothed in Emporio Armani, danced until dawn, while upstairs the stars drank and chatted with Giorgio, who was pleased to offered something new to his city.

That night, Armani had presented his womenswear designs for autumn-winter 1995–1996, an austere but very feminine collection in the colors of mud, sand, and burnished metal, very metropolitan, vertical and linear, pervaded by a nostalgia for the thirties: clinging, with narrow shoulders, an emphatic waistline, long skirts, unpleated trousers, narrow overcoats with velvet lapels. Expansive embroideries and appliqués for the evening wear, with surprising features, such as small bustier, Mao collars for the tuxedoes, and pale pastels. Equally perfect was the press campaign for that season, done by Peter Lindbergh.

Those were the years when the animal rights movement was intensifying its protest activity, gathering outside halls where runway presentations were being held. Armani made a statement establishing his position: "More than twenty years ago I designed a line of furs for an American department store. That was the first and the last time, because I have to say that I am something of an animal rights supporter myself. In my collections, I have never used real fur, and not because I don't like it, but out of a feeling of horror that comes over me when I think of those magnificent animals. Nowadays, moreover, there are fake furs that are soft, light, and look real. In my new collection, I used them as jacket linings or for details." Elaborating on his condemnation of all forms of cruelty and excess, he stated: "Perhaps we could separate what is necessary from what is superfluous: and real fur, as magnificent as it might be, is superfluous." Clear and precise as ever. A dual expression of respect, then, toward animals and women, who deserve better than to wear dead animals. He expressed a logical continuation of this sentiment in an interview for *Panorama* magazine in 1986: "Eating meat strikes me as a form of cannibalism."

Armani's relationship with himself is riddled with conflict: beneath a surface of extreme confidence and self-regard, there lies great fragility and a sort of discontent. He is aware of this split, yet it still provokes behavior that others often misunderstand. He loves adulation and having his way—although he is not good at receiving compliments—but in the end he has greater affection and respect for those who manage to establish a relationship of give-and-take with him, the kind he had with Sergio Galeotti and now has with Leo Dell'Orco: "There is a tacit understanding, which we sometimes forget about, that we never fight in front of others," Dell'Orco tells us. He goes on: "Giorgio is a person who never retreats in the face of the collective. Now, he may think things over afterward and say, 'Yes, you were right.' But in public, his word absolutely has to be the last word. It isn't easy to work with a person like him.... But in the end he is almost always right." Armani is a modern warrior: he loves to battle, to take on the world, to test himself every season even though at this point he could easily be leading a much more relaxed life. His love of a challenge springs from a certain insecurity, yet it is a healthy and vital reaction. "Giorgio is a generous person," says Patrick McCarthy, "and he puts a great deal of passion into everything that he does. He is very competitive, and that is the reason he is so successful. He is willing to compete against anybody, and that makes him a world-class businessman. Because when you begin to think that you are the best, that's when you start to disappear."

Likewise, the attention and care he devotes to his own physical appearance, the discipline he devotes to the battle against the ravages of time, is a challenge to himself rather than the result of vanity. "He is a real health nut," Rosanna Armani tells us, "but with weaknesses typical of the son of the Emilia region that he is. Take him out into the countryside and sit him down in front of a plate of *coppa* cold cuts, and the health nut disappears.... Luckily he has weaknesses! He really cares a lot about his appearance, much more than he used to, and in fact for about ten years now he has been exercising regularly. Actually, after we come home from the holidays, when he sees some of the pictures, he has said to me: 'Either we get into better shape, or you're going to have to stop taking pictures.' And in fact," she goes on, "if you look at photographs of Giorgio from ten years ago, he looked different. My brother doesn't lift weights, he's not a body-builder, but he takes a lot of walks and does exercises without weights, and so his musculature is appropriate to his body." He has a gym and a one-lane lap pool in his house, and exercising has become an unshakable daily habit, even on Sundays and during the summer: "On Pantelleria, he goes out at 7:30 in the morning, and comes back in at 8:45; his trainer is tired, but he is still full of energy. He could outrace a forty-year-old."

By now, discipline is an integral part of his life, as Leo Dell'Orco confirms: "He wakes up at 7:15 and comes in with his blood racing after doing his morning exercises. He finds ten people standing around the coffeemaker and it annoys him. In this aspect, he is very strict, very 'Mussolini-esque.' But I think that this determined attitude of his has allowed him to move forward. I feel certain that whatever he chose to do in life, he would have been successful." He starts his day early and stops for lunch between one and two o'clock in the afternoon; he eats lightly, often with several coworkers, and then restores his energy with a short nap on the couch, just fifteen minutes, in front of the television set. "But he really sleeps deeply!" Dell'Orco points out in amusement. "It is as if he were speed-sleeping through three or four hours of normal sleep." Then he works without a break for the rest of the afternoon and early evening. At eight o'clock he often indulges in an aperitif at Nobu, the Japanese restaurant that has opened up in his megastore on the Via Manzoni. He is astonishingly efficient, and this makes him intolerant of people who can't keep up with him. "He is in the office at 9:15. Of course, young people, nowadays, go out dancing in the evenings, and they might not get in until 9:30. It seemed necessary to me to establish flexible office hours, but it was quite a challenge to succeed in obtaining it. Most people get in at 9:25, and those few minutes during which there is no one at their desks are such a source of irritation to him that he starts yelling," Dell'Orco tell us.

Armani has been described as a narcissist, but really he seems more of an uncompromising perfectionist, an idealist devoted to form, any form: the form of a chair, an easy chair, a landscape, or a body. It is as if by seeking out the essence of things he hopes to extract their inner significance, a higher meaning that would allow him to find peace within his tormented inner world. His is a mystical journey through the realm of all that is most frivolous: appearance. Here is how a great admirer and friend, Patrick McCarthy, describes him:

> One thing that we should say about Giorgio is that he is the hardest-working person that I know. He is obsessed with work. And his look matches his lifestyle. Those impeccable cashmere sweaters, his perfect trousers, his perfect shoes, his perfectly gray hair, his perfect complexion, always perfectly tanned. He is just so perfect, orderly, and disciplined. And everything that he touches is orderly and disciplined. This is the way he works: he works in an orderly and disciplined way, and he never stops. The idea of living upstairs from his offices gives me the idea that he truly is obsessed with his work. It's an old-fashioned way of thinking about life. Even when you go out to dinner with him, there is always a group of his closest colleagues, and they always wind up talking about fashion. Either his fashion or the fashion business in general.

Suzy Menkes, the fashion critic at the *International Herald Tribune*, points out: "Signore Armani never talks much about how hard the war years were, but I believe that he learned a certain work ethic during that period."

In 1995 Armani could be seen seated in the front row at the runway presentation of Dolce and Gabbana, which featured Isabella Rossellini on the catwalk, squeezed into a corset. There was talk, people began to speculate, and he, perfectly aware of what was going on and wryly enjoying it, graciously expressed his appreciation of the energy and verve of the two fashion designers. He also spoke of his respect for other colleagues, such as Issey Miyake, for his artistic talent, and Jean Paul Gaultier, whose creativity he admires. He even voiced doubts about his own inevitable beiges and grays but said he was happy with his work: anyone who chooses to wear Armani must in some sense share his aesthetic and philosophical worldview.

There was more and more discussion of copies and imitations during this period, to the point that in 1995 Pierre Cardin decided not to present his collection because he was so tired of seeing his creations reproduced by American buyers. Giorgio Armani, by this point at the helm of a company with a turnover in 1994 of some 625 billion lire, protected himself from the phenomenon by choosing the more sophisticated, less easy path: "I decided to offer items that were difficult to make, more tailored, if you like. And so, elaborate, careful details, hard to reproduce, like angled cuts. I did my best to personalize my product even more. For me, it was obligatory": an obligation to his customers, who believe they are buying distinction when they buy Armani suits, as well as an obligation to himself and his company. In response to a question designed to put him on the spot, reminding him that he had been one of the first to theorize the democratization of fashion, he said: "Democracy is fine. But there are copies, there is counterfeiting. And that's not okay with me anymore. I design a number of lines, with different price points, for a very diverse public."

The dichotomy between exclusivity and big numbers is a central issue, often unresolved, for all the most important fashion designers and labels. Great arguments raged concerning the term *luxury*, which from this point on would be used endlessly and often inappropriately. Much later—in January 2002—Armani would state that he did not love the word. "By now, even the word *luxury* is disgusting," he went so far as to declare. This declaration, along with others concerning unbridled consumerism in fashion, would inspire pages and pages of reaction from the press: "Armani denounces consumerism, then sells one pair of Armani jeans for 100 pounds sterling," headlined the English daily the *Sunday Telegraph*. But he refused to rise to the provocations and went on as usual (indeed, a couple of years later, he amused himself by inventing Armani Privé, a high-end fashion collection, which will be discussed further in the next chapter). If you are Armani, you can allow yourself the freedom of contradicting yourself or, in any case, following your own personal logic. And Giorgio, at the age of sixty-one, was at the summit of his career—a somewhat tardy achievement, by ordinary standards. In fact, in a conversation with Giorgio Bocca, he had an opportunity to recall a slightly bitter exchange with his mother: "You see, Mamma, now we have everything." "Yes, Giorgio, but a little late."

In those years, the relationship between advertising and fashion reporting was increasingly intertwined. *Vogue*, *Harper's Bazaar*, and other magazines would represent a designer's work in proportion to how many pages of advertising he or she purchased. The same held true for reviews of a runway presentation in daily newspapers. The years of spontaneous coverage were over, and a subjective, manipulated press made it difficult even for fashion designers themselves to gain objective estimations of their own merits and flaws by means of honest criticism. Nonetheless, Armani remained the king. He knew how to evolve and what the world wanted from him. Among the many areas where he was ahead of his time, he had an understanding, long before his colleagues, of the importance of a page of advertising in the daily press. As early as 1985, for example, for the tenth anniversary of the Giorgio Armani company, he bought ten pages of advertising in *La Repubblica*; for the same edition, the most respected journalists on the paper interviewed Giorgio and Sergio Galeotti for a story about the company. On another occasion, he bought all the advertising space of a single issue of the news weekly *Panorama*. At the end of the nineties, the strategy intensified, extending to the entire advertising section of many international dailies and weeklies. "The idea of filling up entire issues of the most prestigious publications at certain times of the year dates back many years," Armani declared in 1998, "and it is a way of creating a powerful image that raises your profile above what is known as the fashion ghetto." In fall 1997 he took over the Style insert of *The New York Times Magazine*; in March 1998 came the special issue for the seventy-fifth anniversary of the Atlantic edition of *Time*, which reaches more than 625,000 readers in Europe, Africa, and the Middle East. Also in 1998 he purchased entire issues of *L'Espresso, Il Sole 24 Ore, La Repubblica,* and *La Repubblica*'s women's supplement, *D*. It was all Armani advertising in an entire issue of *Il Corriere della Sera* and its supplement, *Sette*; of the then weekly magazine *Amica*; and the Sunday supplement of the Belgian daily *Die Standard*. The same scheme was carried out with *Le Monde*, in the issue corresponding to the inauguration of the Saint Germain Emporio Armani.

Street advertising also became increasingly important, for instance, the mural that for the past ten years or so has held pride of place in the center of Milan, transforming the corner of the Via Broletto and changing people's habits. The giant image of Emporio Armani has become a rendezvous point for people meeting in the area. "I believe that I was the first to put such faith in the mural. Followed by Benetton and by others in the course of time. For that matter, I had borrowed the idea from Calvin Klein who had made an enormous mural on Broadway, with a pair of his underwear. If I think of my mural with the cobblestones and the bicycle in the Via Broletto [one of the most popular subjects featured] in this context," he continues, "I no longer consider it as a personal exhibition but rather as the need to interpret my work in a way that no one else could do: a wet cobblestone street, a bicycle wheel with a red cat's-eye reflector, the Armani logo, the only bit of color in the entire poster. As if to say: an exceptional element in everyday life, a solid lifestyle, reliable values. And that is why I increasingly see this spreading need among a number of companies to put their name on their own image and to build their own 'corporate image' through editorial instruments: we produce two each year, *Giorgio Armani* and *Emporio Armani Magazine*, which ensure, we hope, a message that accurately reflects the substance of the work we are doing." When a journalist asked him whether he had ever thought of founding a new magazine or underwriting one, he responded confidently: "For my work, I prefer to be able to rely on all the media, instead of being tied to a single medium. Press and television bring the whole world to me: music, movies, soccer championships, great catastrophes, wars, tourism, vacations, big stars, F1 racing, the America's Cup. All those collective events that for a fashion creator have the value and weight of gigantic live market research."

Armani stated in an interview with the Italian advertising trade publication *Prima Comunicazione* that he invests about 5 percent of his induced revenue in advertising. And so in 1994, out of about 1.3 trillion lire, he spent about 60 billion on advertising: "That's about right, with advertising, promotion, and runway presentations. We also invest a significant chunk on market research proper." Although he claims no standing as an expert in sociology or contemporary anthropology, Armani is very insightful and discriminating: "Often, the message that comes from society, as well as from the world of fashion itself, is so powerful or vulgar that it prompts a closing off inside me, a rejection of that message, and the decision to exclude it from my work, as well as from the 'methods' of my fashion. When I see that military fashion, or Chinese fashion, or anything else, is rising up to become a harsh, overwhelming message, then I pull back from it. In that overly harsh message I smell rhetoric, mass style, and even violence. I hate being in the crowd, that's not my way, that's not the essence of the work I do. I have to propose stylistic innovation, new forms of imagination and behavior. I don't want to be dragged into the din of shocks and scoops, the fake revolutions. That is also why," he went on, "I don't much like all the noise made about top models: I don't like having my clothing worn by Claudia Schiffer, who also bares her ass. Because then people look at her ass, not at my clothing."

Often, in those contradictory years, so heavily influenced by fashion, the press referred to fashion designers as mere tailors. Armani was spared this sniping, yet he commented on how poorly the word describes what he does: "I don't mind being called a tailor, but I don't like the lie: I wasn't born a tailor, and I wouldn't know how to be a tailor. My professional training was, first of all, in fabric technology and later, as a designer for the clothing industry. Of course, after all the fittings I have done with seamstresses working on prototypes for the Giorgio Armani company, I can quickly figure out how to eliminate a defect, bring a shoulder up or down, take in a bulge. But it's all theoretical. I don't even know how to hold a needle." He is a very skillful draftsman, though. His sketches, the ones he draws before putting together each collection, provide extraordinary syntheses, and with a few expert lines he depicts not only the outfit in all its slightest details but the very spirit it is meant to convey.

Among his other virtues, Armani rightly claims that he has always avoided being an opinion maker. There was a time in the nineties when fashion designers were asked to pronounce on anything and everything, as if, just because they were famous, they had the right to expound on existential topics. But he, very properly, said: "Women don't want 'knowledge' from me, they just want to 'have' clothing that reassures them, clothing that preserves a continuous meaning over time. What they ask of me is a sort of 'nonbetrayal.' " Loyal to the line, even in his most recent collections, Armani does not yield to the temptations of transparent materials and exaggerated curves: "I chose a specific approach because I believe that everyone has to do that. I created a small niche for myself and I think that it is incumbent upon me to continue to believe in it, because no matter what, the results that my style has brought me are always very positive. The day that I realize that my product is no longer selling well, I will consider myself to be behind the times, and I will admit that I need to change. But whenever I jump the tracks a little bit, I hear everyone say it to me, both the press and the customers: this is not like you, that's not what we want and expect from you." The dividing line between himself and his fashion is increasingly faint, although this certainly doesn't denote any immobility: "Creating a cliché for yourself forces you, to some extent, always to be yourself. It's a risk; but it's also an advantage, because you know that the variations on a theme will never do much to undermine your sales. Another risk: letting your own style get old on you, becoming a ham and turning into a caricature of yourself. And that is why, over the past few years, I have made lots of changes in my ideas about my fashion, and I make clothing that may be very feminine indeed, evening gowns, for instance." In a world that is stripping away the last shreds of the halo of magic that once surrounded femininity, he offers a sophisticated and personal interpretation of that concept so eternally, irremediably baffling to one and all: "If we talk about a sexy look, there is a vast misunderstanding. Generally speaking, people use *sexy* to mean a style that reveals or shows off. I think that *sexy* is something different: for instance, a woman revealing a little of her bosom beneath a man's jacket. The sex appeal that most people talk about is much more open and much cheaper. Instead, I think showing your breasts isn't sexy, I think little gestures that women make are sexy. The way they cross their legs, how they turn up their lapels or uncover an arm. I try to avoid the obvious, the cheap, the garish, the excessively simple, clear, or facile. On the contrary, I want to send subtler messages to my audience, I want to allow people to live as freely as they wish with the clothing that I offer." Giorgio Armani proudly reinforces his position among the opposition:

> Let's just say right away that I have always gone against the prevailing current. I have always been astonished by

this trend, which began quietly, of showing off fashion models instead of clothing, the emphasis on personalities, the conditioning that was in part due to the members of the profession: photographers, hairstylists, and fashion editors, who have frequently been involved in a fairly substantial way in the editing of the collections. Perhaps I've just been unusually lucky: from the initial sketches to the staging of the runway presentation, I have always been directly involved in every aspect of the process. But it's easier for me than delegating. If I make a mistake, then it's my mistake; if I set myself up on a pedestal, then I'm there through my own efforts, straightforward and honest. But if we're talking about the articles that appear in the daily press, thirty lines long, more than half of them are devoted to the society event and not the clothing being presented. And I think that's crazy. This work we do is serious work, very demanding. To see six months' worth of insanely intense work summed up in a commentary on the fact that at the runway presentation of this fashion designer one of the top models was angry is just humiliating. Yes, I believe that we have reached the brink of chaos. I believe that the time has come for a return to professional behavior.

In 1996 Giorgio's brother, Sergio, the father of Silvana and Roberta Armani, died. He was in a Milanese hospital for treatment, and one night his life simply ended, a life in which flashes of euphoria, in which he expressed all his creativity, alternated with moments of equally great darkness. "In many ways we were very similar," Armani said a few years later (as usual he hid his pain from the spotlights of the press). "But he lacked my ability to keep my feet firmly planted on the ground. He really was an extremist. He suffered from terrible states of depression, and I think that in the end his heart just gave out."

That same year, the Giorgio Armani company moved its press and styling offices to the much-sought-after Palazzo Orsini at Via Borgonuovo 11, purchased in 1993 for 65 billion lire. Until 1990 the property and headquarters of the Associazione Cotoniera Italiana (Italian cotton manufacturers' association), the building dates from the end of the sixteenth century and boasts a neoclassical facade rebuilt by Luigi Clerichetti in the mid-nineteenth century. The oval wardrobe on the main floor was decorated by Andrea Appiani in the second half of the eighteenth century. The Renaissance courtyard is exceptionally harmonious, and the garden borders the Orto Botanico (Botanical Gardens) of the Via Brera. The administrative offices are at number 18, directly across the street. And at number 21 Giorgio Armani still has his home and the little auditorium for runway presentations.

On the occasion of the twenty-fifth anniversary of Pitti Immagine Uomo, Luigi Settembrini, a fashion historian and one of the directors of the Florence-based fashion event, dreamed up a project that would be the talk of the industry. "G.A. Story" was set in the Stazione Leopolda, a former train station in Florence newly renovated by the architect Gae Aulenti, and it featured clothing by Giorgio Armani and a spectacular mise-en-scène designed by Robert Wilson. The famed American theatrical director "narrated, in a four-thousand-square-meter [forty-three-thousand-square-foot] space, with ten sections, and with a horde of dances, mimes, and clothes models, video installations, forests of birch trees, labyrinths of laurel, two stages, and musical compositions for wind, violin, and power saw, or for ocean waves, horns, and helicopter, and of course with heaps and heaps of clothes, the life and the work of Giorgio Armani, the highest-earning Italian designer on earth: 1.4 trillion lire," as Natalia Aspesi summarized the event in *La Repubblica*.

The event was produced by Pitti Immagine and staged twice: The inaugural show was held on June 21 for heads of state and government who had gathered in Florence from all over Europe for a summit conference of the European Union. The second performance, on the evening of Wednesday, July 3, was staged for fashion professionals, who were flabbergasted by the spectacular ninety-minute show (a very short production for a director known for operas that last anywhere from ten hours to three days). It was an encounter of two powerful personalities: "Fashion is an important form of expression of contemporary imagery," Wilson said, "because on a stage, a piece of clothing has the same visual value as a chair, as much meaning as a text, every bit as much significance as a sound, and conveys as much emotion as a gesture: it can express speed and slowness, it can give meaning to space and time, all themes that form part of my own body of expressive work." And he added: "I believe that I share with Armani a passion for details, a striving for perfection, and a mania for simplicity, for purity. I like his fashion because it is relaxed, it is the product of a research, an absolute dedication. It is the most complete idea of clothing nowadays."

When someone asked Giorgio Armani how he was managing to suppress his need to supervise every last detail, the fashion designer responded: "Let's just say that not being able to control an event that is about me was something of an ordeal. But the one luxury that I can afford nowadays is to risk:

abandoning for once the traditional runway presentation, entrusting myself to the genius of another person, and, concerning my menswear for the summer of 1997, which I utilized to dress the twenty-two dancers and the twenty male models (plus twelve female dancers and twenty-one female models), I insisted on presenting a normal, unexaggerated style of clothing." This courageous undertaking inevitably drew some subtle barbs, especially from the pragmatic American buyers. Kal Ruttenstein of Bloomingdale's commented: "I went to Florence to see clothing, and I'm a little disappointed that I wasn't able to see it." He added: "It really was beautiful. Everybody said that it was, including people who were very beautiful themselves, and so I have to believe it really was beautiful."

Once again, America applauded Armani. The opening of a new Emporio Armani and a Giorgio Armani boutique in New York offered an opportunity for memorable celebrations, followed as usual by the inevitable polemics. The building designed and built by Peter Marino, a huge white cube looming over Madison Avenue, was poorly proportioned according to a number of detractors, who also criticized a general poverty of details and the fact that it seems completely out of character with the section of the city where it is located. Four stories of bright white limestone enclosing approximately seventeen thousand square feet, with a café and restaurant on the bottom floor, it was certainly a substantial investment. Regardless of the criticism it inspired, it won the enthusiastic approval of the seven hundred illustrious guests who showed up for the opening bash at the Manhattan Armory, a former military structure transformed for the evening into an elegant night club hosting performances by the Fugees, Eric Clapton, Jakob Dylan and the Wallflowers, and the dancer Joaquín

Cortés. The assembled actors and other celebrities once again provided testimonials of their respect and fondness for Giorgio Armani. The fashion designer was still recognized as the most important, supreme in his field, even if he now shared the stage with Prada and Gucci (about whom he still has some reservations). His new American venture was just another confirmation of that fact. The most popular department stores in New York (Barneys, Bergdorf Goodman, Saks Fifth Avenue, and Bloomingdale's) devoted their display windows to his winter collections for an entire week, and the magazine publishing house Condé Nast wallpapered Manhattan with posters welcoming the two new stores.

In September of the same year, in Florence, a new Pitti Immagine project was inaugurated: the first edition of the Biennale. "Il Tempo e la Moda" (Time and fashion) was a challenge, a promotional relaunching of the city and Italian fashion. Culturally diverse, it was a crucible in which a great many ingredients were mingled together. The intention was to provide a narrative of the influences and exchanges linking all the visual arts, including fashion, of course, which emerged from the confrontation a little drained of color, a little bit a prisoner of itself. A corner in the first corridor of the Galleria degli Uffizi was set aside for Giorgio Armani. "It was a very positive and encouraging experience for me," Armani later declared. "There might have been a few things that needed retouching, and that goes for what I did as well. I believe that the Biennale has acquired a stature and an importance that I didn't expect at first. If there is another opportunity of this sort, I'll be more careful next time." The experience prompted some reflection: "It is a consolation to think that you can still come out of your own shell, have some courage, and take on new things, try out new ways of doing things. When I walked into the Uffizi, I asked myself: What am I doing here, even if I do make beautiful clothing? I believe that I am being attributed qualities and virtues to an excessive degree. And then, bit by bit, on tiptoe, in a very discreet and cautious manner, and without overdoing it, suggesting only my own style and colors, I began to move among artworks of inestimable value."

Armani's eye for beauty could not help giving him a special sensitivity to art: "I feel an incredible attraction for Hokusai and for the gentle landscapes that Hiroshige Hitsu painted toward the middle of the nineteenth century. But what really fascinated me were the hybrids, the cross-fertilization, the new ideas: for instance, *La Japonaise*, which Monet exhibited at the second Salon of the Impressionists, but also the stupendous series of the *Water Lilies*, done over thirty years later. Manet, Degas, and Van Gogh were also at the intersection between the West and Japanese influences, at a time when Hiroshige was so famous in Europe that Van Gogh was a dedicated collector of his prints." This passion led him to sponsor, in February 1996, a major exhibition of work by the impressionists, held at the Palazzo Reale in Milan. In the collection he showed in March of that year, there was an echo of Matisse: "I was inspired by him for my evening gowns," Armani said, admitting that Matisse's painting *The Goldfish* had stimulated him to convert to color, at least for that season.

Art influences his work, but only indirectly. Armani cares deeply about distinguishing different genres and disciplines, and in response to the eternal question of whether fashion is art, he replies with a decisive no. "In my view, making fashion means designing a wearable outfit, which lets a person who wears it feel comfortable, at ease." Aside from his general fascination with form, however, it is evident that he carries out relentless and meticulous research into color: "One of my first concerns, when I design a collection, is the palette of colors. Quite often, I am unable to find those nuances and shades in the fabrics that already exist. Because I imagined them myself, establishing a deep-seated relationship between my sketches and the colors. The sketches and the colors work together to provide a form and an identity that is all the more powerful and determined the less it needs to entrust itself to the provisional vehicle of splash and astonishment. I am well known for my predilection for soft, neutral shades. When I select a color, even if it's black, lilac, or turquoise, I want it to be filtered, look lived in, as it were. Rarely am I seduced by a pure shade, which I find excessively crude and, all things considered, simplistic." And he talks about his youthful love of oil painting: "I would happily spend an entire day in front of a canvas," he recalls. "I was good at copying. I would imitate Modigliani's long-necked women, and I even redid a small Caravaggio. Then I gave it up, but it influenced my later work a great deal. The color research that I did, for example." Many simplistically describe as minimalism his well-known taste for the purity of line, for the essence of things, for form and volume. "Minimalism is a part of my nature, of the way I live, the food I eat, and the way I spread out my appearances in society. And it has been, since the beginning of my career, also a banner of my style, dense with content and devoid of useless substrates," Armani states but then goes on to explain: "The error into which one falls all too often when talking about a minimalist conception of fashion lies in confusing simplicity and banality, for instance, believing that a shabby-looking miniskirt and sweater are an ethical message within the context of aesthetic research, while often they are merely the birth of minimalism taken as a trend rather than a stylistic conception, as an ecology of form rather than of substance and therefore a product of the mind." Often Armani has expressed himself through exercises that were actually virtuosic explorations of the theme of decoration: he has presented evening gowns encrusted with beads, crystals, and passementerie. He has designed skirts and outfits that were delicate and nuanced, exquisite as Chinese porcelains, like Japanese screens. He has a distinctive manner of distilling the signs of other cultures, simplifying them and rendering their essence. He has always succeeded in filtering his inspirations and carefully calibrating them. It is more a process of interiorizing an idea than an explicit reference. It is a little like what happened to the avant-garde artists.

In June 1997 Roberta Armani, Giorgio's beautiful niece, the younger sister of Silvana, married Angelo Moratti, the young scion of a major family of the Milanese bourgeoisie. Roberta had been working for the family company for three years. She started out as a liaison to the foreign press, and now she was in charge of promotion for Emporio Armani. Her role became increasingly significant, and, aside from supervising relations between the Giorgio Armani company and various celebrities, she worked alongside her uncle on all public events. In part, this was because of her good English, because even though Giorgio Armani understands the language, he cannot speak it.

In the summer of 1997, the world was shaken by the sudden death of Gianni Versace, Giorgio Armani's great rival. Versace was a fashion designer whose authentic talent Armani acknowledged but with whom, at first, he did not have a very close relationship. "Both of them were pretty hostile to each other," Adriana Mulassano remembers, "and they were also suspicious. They had not yet understood that they were so different from each other that they would never enter onto a collision course on stylistic grounds. When they began to understand that each of them was going his separate way, things settled down." Armani was shaken by Gianni Versace's death; he had come to think of him as a sort of alter ego, "the half that he was not and that he did not possess." He thought of Versace almost as a complementary part of him. There is a picture of Armani walking into the Milan Duomo: his face is drawn, and he is wearing a dark suit and running shoes. He has chosen the stairs of a side entrance in order to avoid the crowd that has gathered in front of the great cathedral, seemingly vying for entrance to a society event rather than what was instead a memorial mass for Gianni Versace.

The Asian markets were some of the most active in the nineties, and they especially favored Italian fashion designers. In Milan, the shops of the fashion district teemed with Japanese shoppers purchasing, photographing, and strolling as they tried their best to absorb as much European spirit as possible. The Giorgio Armani Japan company in 1996 had a turnover of some 250 billion lire. In November of the following year Armani returned to Japan for the first time in about fifteen years. Tokyo gave him an imperial welcome. Posters hung everywhere in the city, emblazoned with his portrait and announcing the runway presentation that would be held in the Meiji Park, across from the Kaigakan Museum, in two black pavilions built in just a few days to house no fewer than twelve hundred contented guests while a live television broadcast allowed the Japanese viewing audience to watch the proceedings. A few years later, Armani entered the Chinese market as well, inaugurating his first boutique in Beijing: forty-eight hundred square feet inside the Palace Hotel.

The Giorgio Armani company's policy of expansion continued at an unbroken pace and, while the largest A/X Armani Exchange shop was being opened in New York, along with two Giorgio Armani boutiques in Las Vegas and one in Kobe, Japan, in Paris the large Emporio Armani shop in the Boulevard Saint Germain opened its doors. It replaced the historic Le Drugstore, in one of the best-loved sections of the city, an ousting that would trigger a number of controversies. A committee was even founded to defend the quarter's identity: it voiced the general sense of concern over the loss of an invaluable cultural resource, a place where it had been possible, at three in the morning, to purchase the latest book by Bernard-Henri Lévy. Juliette Gréco exclaimed, "They have destroyed Saint Germain," but then changed her mind after visiting the new space, which soon became a much frequented and beloved location. It didn't hurt that Giorgio Armani had also paid to restore the stained glass windows of the cathedral of Saint Germain.

To celebrate the opening of the new space, an Emporio Armani runway presentation in Paris was planned for March 1998. The project was complex but still reasonably routine. Giorgio Armani had met Pierre Bergé, the founder of the Chambre Syndicale du Prêt-à-porter and the president of the Maison Saint Laurent, who many years before had indulged in a sarcastic critique of Italian fashion in general and Armani's in particular. Now Bergé welcomed him enthusiastically. "Giorgio received all the permits to erect an enormous tensile structure in the Place Saint-Sulpice, and in that structure he was going to hold his runway presentation and host a dinner," recalls Adriana Mulassano, who was an eyewitness to the whole affair. "We had been in Paris for twenty days to organize everything, and every morning a representative of the

Gendarmerie would come by to ensure that the work was being done properly. Everything was in compliance, but at two in the afternoon on the day of the event, with the models already getting made up, the chief of police came in, took a look around, and told us that we couldn't hold the runway presentation: there were supposed to be seventeen emergency exits, and we only had sixteen. We reassured him and told him that we would make another emergency exit immediately: the runway presentation was scheduled for nine o'clock, we had all the time we needed." But the authorities were immovable. The Paris Préfecture de Police declared that the structure "presented major shortcomings in relation to the regulatory requirements imposed by the presence of twelve hundred persons" and forbade the runway presentation at the very last second. "And in that situation, I think that Giorgio was divine," Mulassano continued. "He proved that he was someone special, because he decided to just go ahead and hold the runway presentation all the same, with the doors closed, and all the guests left outside, and the only audience was the people who had worked with him. There was no audience, in other words, but there was still a runway presentation. And most important of all, the whole time, Giorgio never lost his temper." Everything went off smoothly, but only for the benefit of the Armani staff: "It was like a movie," recalls Roberta Armani, "with the staff applauding thunderously, tears of pride and disappointment streaming down their cheeks. The dinner was donated to the Paris homeless." *Le Nouvel Observateur* quoted Armani's calm reaction: "I am disappointed and shocked. I was profoundly struck by the manner in which the French authorities handled the whole matter. There has always been a rivalry between France and Italy, but there are bounds beyond which you simply do not go. Sometimes, you have to remain a human being. It has always been a great challenge for an Italian to win the Tour de France, and when it finally happened, as Paolo Conte sang in one of his songs: the French have their balls still spinning as a result." When someone asked him if he would ever come back to Paris for a runway presentation, he smiled and responded: "Certainly, I love war, I fight a new war every day!"

The incident, clearly sparked by partisan politics and, in the view of many people, symptomatic of a profound jealousy, prompted reactions from such illustrious colleagues as Paco Rabanne, who declared: "It's indecent. An insult to Armani, but also to the rest of us. What they've killed is Paris's standing as the capital of fashion." Lagerfeld, too, decided to make a show of solidarity: "I want to express my sympathy for Armani, I am ashamed of the decision made by the French police, and I deplore this terrible example of French chauvinism." And Pierre Bergé took this opportunity to say: "Armani is a great couturier. I am deeply shocked." There survives from that evening a moving interview recorded in the basement of the Hotel Ritz. No complaints, only a great regret expressed without ever turning into rancor.

He decided to turn to the United States as an alternative: "After that experience, there were no options left open to me except to show the Emporio Armani collection in New York, during fashion week. They immediately welcomed me, without problems," Giorgio Armani commented. Rudolph Giuliani, then the mayor of New York, insisted on meeting privately with him in the Blue Room of City Hall; the two men exchanged gifts, and Giuliani thanked Armani for all that he had done for the city (at the time, at least a thousand people were working for the

Giorgio Armani company in the United States, in twelve Emporio Armani shops, nine Giorgio Armani boutiques, and twenty-six retail outlets for menswear and menswear in American department stores). Armani, tired of feeling like a tourist in New York, allowed himself to be persuaded by his friends Liam Neeson and his wife, Natasha Richardson, to purchase an apartment overlooking Central Park, next door to the famous Dakota apartment house, where John Lennon had lived.

Eight hundred guests attended the runway presentation. "I wanted to make my young women stronger, more aggressive, a girl who no longer sees herself as an adolescent, childish, but rather, adult and mature, even if she is still young," as Armani tells it. "I like to think for winter of a woman who renders herself precious, not by uncovering herself, but enveloping herself in trousers, jackets, blouses, soft and fluttering, beneath which the body is not uncovered." And fifty-six female models, wearing opalescent makeup, to the cadenced rhythm of the runway music, presented images that some believe were inspired by the protagonists of *Memoirs of a Geisha*, the novel on which the 2006 movie was based (a film that Armani would later present in a sneak preview in his theater on the Via Bergognone in Milan), although the idea of seduction entrusted to mystery has always been a favorite theme of the fashion designer's. The runway presentation was followed by the inevitable dinner, with the most illustrious names in cinema as guests, from Martin Scorsese and Spike Lee to Sophia Loren (accompanied by her son Edoardo) and Robert De Niro.

"The first reaction was humility, considering the company I was keeping." That is what Giorgio Armani said in acknowledgment of yet another recognition from *Time* magazine, which in June 1998 listed him among the top hundred personalities of the century in art, literature, and entertainment. He was the only Italian, aside from Luigi Pirandello, and was in the company of Joyce, Le Corbusier, Picasso, the Beatles, and Chaplin. "Then, above all, I felt a sense of satisfaction. I heard the news when I was in New York, and the city has never looked so good to me! I really am happy, even though this will certainly fuel debates and the inevitable jealousies. But that's how it should be: everything is a matter of opinion, and everyone can see things as they like."

The Giorgio Armani S.p.A. continued to dominate the top rankings: it employed twenty-five hundred people, and it was the most profitable Italian company. By this point it could look back on a long and dense history, and yet it had grown "without any specific plan," as the managing director, Giuseppe Brusone, would admit. At the end of the nineties, in fact, it became necessary to equip the company with "a structure that was in keeping with the levels attained by the group, with the ultimate goal of separating the four activities of industry, retail, licensing and royalties, and style consulting," a wide-ranging and complex corporate restructuring that according to Brusone's plans was intended to lead to a second phase where it would be necessary either to be quoted on the stock exchange or else to seek out a strategic alliance with a strong partner. "I am sixty-four years old and I realize that the time will come when I will feel ridiculous getting up on the runway and taking the applause following a runway presentation, with both hands in the air and wearing the usual dark-blue T-shirt. I have a pretty strong sense of self-criticism and, therefore, I am preparing myself for that moment," Armani said in an interview with *Il Sole 24 Ore* in October 1998. "I could imagine a development of the company toward a family operation, but I have no children of my own, and my nieces, even though they work with me, would never be willing to take on commitments at that level. There are three possible solutions: selling outright, selling in part, or being on the stock exchange. There are commercial banks lined up outside the door, and they would shower me with gold, but money isn't a factor in this decision: I would never have enough time to spend it. Or else I could limit the work I am doing to styling without having anything to do with the management of the company itself. We'll see. In no more than three or four years I will have to decide. In the meantime, I'll just wish for good luck and wait."

While fear of the millennium bug seeped into the minds of the masses, the fashion world was more excited by acquisitions than by innovations in style, as evidenced by the mass media's fascination with the takeover battle between LVMH and the Pinault-Printemps-Redoute Group for control of Gucci. But Giorgio Armani, as he reflected on the fate of his own corporation, followed more than economic criteria. "People really like to know who they are working with and who they are working for," he said. "They see me come in at nine in the morning and leave at eight in the evening, from the postman who says hello to me as he passes by to an entire excellent staff of designers. Maybe I'm just a little too sentimental. Maybe I'll have to lose some of that sentimental attitude in 2000." In February 1999 Bernard Arnault, president of LVMH, the major luxury goods group, was seen seated in the front row at the presentation of the menswear collection. This fomented a great hubbub among journalists, who claimed to have known for some time now that negotiations were under way. In the end nothing happened: official sources denied the allegations, and the name Armani would not join the list of Dior, Givenchy, and Lacroix, already part of the most important French fashion stable. The company would remain independent. Armani had built an empire around his own prickly and authoritarian image, he has a strong sense of family, and he rejects the cynical approach to business that no longer takes into account the personality at the center of the question. "I am happy that we have managed to create a credible and successful business," he told Suzy Menkes in 1999 in an interview for the *International Herald Tribune*. "Right now there are a great many proposals and possibilities with three or four groups, but I am not obliged to find a partner. We have plenty of money for all our future plans, with no need to seek out investors. It is a decision that should be weighed carefully. My work is my life. Even if it is nice to take holidays, after some time off, you get bored. And it would be difficult not to be independent. I am used to making my decisions on my own. It would be complicated to choose a potential partner. Perhaps impossible."

In via Durini 24 (1976).

Giorgio Armani at work.
Top, left and right: In via Durini 24.
Bottom: In via Borgonuovo 21.
Opposite: Giorgio Armani at his worktable. Photo © Graziella Vigo

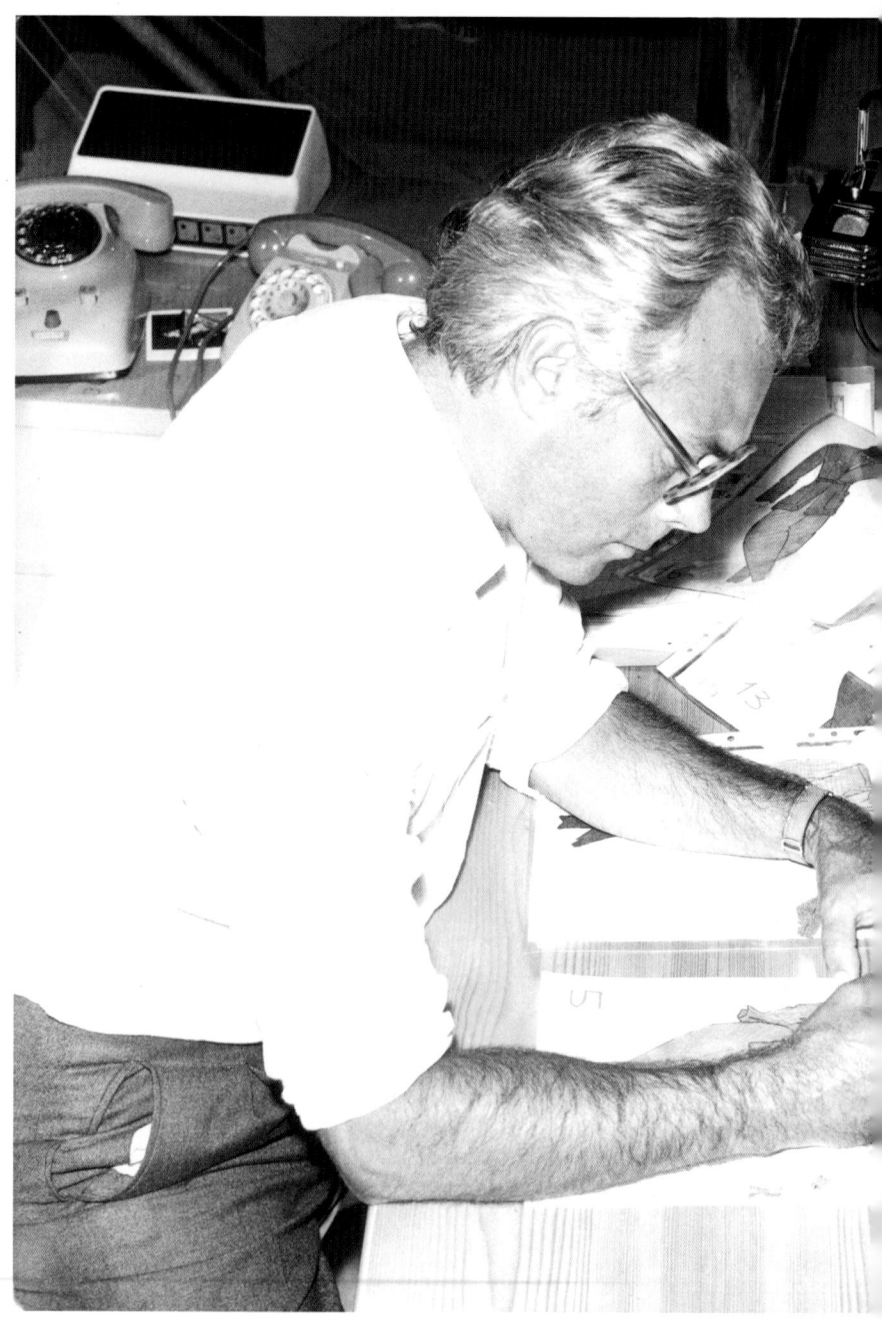

At the worktable with the latest designs for a collection.

Top: Rosanna, Giorgio, and Silvana Armani in via Borgonuovo 21. Photo © Graziella Vigo
Bottom: Giorgio with his nieces Silvana and Roberta.

Sergio Galeotti in a photo shoot for *L'Uomo Vogue* on his Triumph. Photo © Carlo Orsi

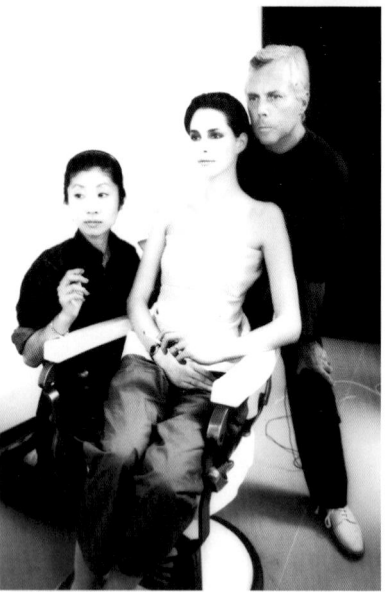

Technical rehearsals in preparation for a collection.
Top left: The fitting. Photo © Arnaldo Liverani
Top right: From *Made in Milan* by Martin Scorsese (1990). Photo © Gastone Jung
Bottom left: Last-minute adjustments before the fashion show. Photo © Gastone Jung
Bottom right: Final touches to the makeup. Photo © Gastone Jung
Opposite: Giorgio Armani with Leo Dell'Orco after a fashion show.

Some designs by Giorgio Armani.

Photo © Roger Hutchings

Giorgio Armani Men's Collection.
Top left: Spring-Summer collection 1975.
Top right: Spring-Summer collection 1976.
Bottom left: Autumn-Winter collection 1979/80.
Bottom right: Autumn-Winter collection 1982/83.
Photo © Aldo Fallai

Giorgio Armani Men's Collection.
Top left: Spring-Summer collection 1984.
Top right: Autumn-Winter collection 1985/86.
Bottom left: Autumn-Winter collection 1989/90.
Bottom right: Spring-Summer collection 1991.
Photo © Aldo Fallai

Giorgio Armani Women's Collection.
Top left: Autumn-Winter collection 1980/81.
Top right: Autumn-Winter collection 1981/82.
Bottom left: Autumn-Winter collection 1982/83. Photo © Aldo Fallai
Bottom right: Autumn-Winter collection 1993/94. Photo © Enrique Badulescu
Opposite page: Autumn-Winter collection 1990/91. Photo © Jacques Olivar
From *Emporio Armani Magazine.*

From *Emporio Armani Magazine*.
Top left: Autumn-Winter collection 1993/94. Photo © Jacques Olivar
Top right: Spring-Summer collection 1996. Photo © Aldo Fallai
Bottom left: Autumn-Winter collection 1996/97. Photo © Marino Parisotto
Giorgio Armani Men's Collection.
Bottom right: Autumn-Winter collection 2002/2003. Photo © Paolo Roversi
Opposite: Spring-Summer collection 2003. Testimonial Oliver Martinez. Photo © Paolo Roversi

Giorgio Armani Women's Collection.
Top, both: **Spring-Summer collection 1989.** Photo © Aldo Fallai
Bottom left: **Autumn-Winter collection 1992/93.** Photo © Peter Lindbergh
Bottom right: **Spring-Summer collection 1993.** Photo © Peter Lindbergh
Opposite: **Autumn-Winter collection 1990/91.** Photo © Aldo Fallai

Giorgio Armani Men's Collection.
Top left: Autumn-Winter collection 1990/91. Photo © Aldo Fallai
Top right: Autumn-Winter collection 1994/95. Photo © Peter Lindbergh
Bottom left: Spring-Summer collection 1995. Photo © Peter Lindbergh
Bottom right: Spring-Summer collection 1996. Photo © Peter Lindbergh

Giorgio Armani Men's Collection.
Top left: Spring-Summer collection 1997. Photo © Paolo Roversi
Top right: Spring-Summer collection 1998. Photo © Aldo Fallai
Bottom left: Spring-Summer collection 2002. Photo © Peter Lindbergh
Armani Collezioni Men's Collection.
Bottom right: Autumn-Winter collection 2006/2007. Photo © Aldo Fallai

Giorgio Armani Women's Collection.
Top left: Spring-Summer collection 2002. Photo © Peter Lindbergh
Top right: Autumn-Winter collection 2002/2003. Photo © Paolo Roversi
Bottom left: Spring-Summer collection 2003. Photo © Paolo Roversi
Armani Collezioni Women's Collection.
Bottom right: Autumn-Winter collection 2006/07. Photo © Aldo Fallai
Giorgio Armani Women's Collection.
Opposite: Autumn-Winter collection 1996/97. Photo © Peter Lindbergh

Giorgio Armani Privé Couture Collection, Autumn-Winter 2006/2007.
Photo © Piero Biasion.

Giorgio Armani extends his thanks.

Photo © Sergio Caminata

Jodie Foster, Michelle Pfeiffer, Dustin Hoffman, Ashley Judd

Demi Moore, Ornella Muti, Fanny Ardant

Samuel L. Jackson, Sophia Loren, Christina Aguilera

Isabella Rossellini, Jennifer Aniston, Claudia Cardinale

Winona Ryder, Sting, Trudie Styler, Uma Thurman

Tom Hanks, Mira Sorvino, Eva Green

Pierce Brosnan, Anne Parillaud, George H. W. Bush

Clint Eastwood, Laura Morante, Tom Cruise

Matt Dillon, Faye Dunaway, Kim Basinger, Sigourney Weaver

Kaká, Lemar, Andy Warhol

Woody Allen, Nick Lachey, Jessica Simpson, will.I.Am

Debbie Mazar, King Juan Carlos of Spain, Usher

Pope John Paul II, Spike Lee, Michael Keaton

Vittoria Belvedere, Christian Slater, Bill and Hillary Clinton, Oscar Luigi Scalfaro

Mike Figgis, Eric Clapton, Leonardo DiCaprio

Dee Dee Bridgewater, Gwyneth Paltrow, Ben Affleck, Mickey Rourke

Alessandra Martines, Claude Lelouch, Sonia Braga, Lauren Bacall

Lee Radziwill, Princess Caroline of Monaco, Robert De Niro, Martin Scorsese

Isabelle Huppert, Andy Garcia, Antonio Banderas, Marion Cotillard

Bernardo Bertolucci, Kristin Scott Thomas, Raoul Bova, Silvio Muccino

Charlie Sheen, Denise Richards, John Travolta, Martin Scorsese

Chiara Muti, Andriy Shevchenko, Richard Gere, Joaquín Cortés

Jeanne Tripplehorn, Ben Stiller, George Clooney, Kevin Spacey

Beyoncé, Claudia Cardinale, Sophia Loren, Demi Moore, Lauren Hutton

Lucio Dalla, Natasha Richardson, Liam Neeson, Russell Crowe

Barbra Streisand, Anjelica Huston, Donald Sutherland

Michael Jackson, Andrea Camerana, Christopher Lambert, Val Kilmer

Harrison Ford, Calista Flockhart, Glenn Close

Jeremy Irons, Ashley Judd, Kevin Kline, Lyle Lovett

Cécile De France, Gerard Butler, Brad Pitt, George Clooney

Tadao Ando, Jack Nicholson, Silvio Muccino

Gillo Pontecorvo, Sharon Stone, Rudolph Giuliani

CHAPTER NINE

Thinking of the Future

People still travel by car, train, and plane; the spaceships that were predicted for the year 2000 exist only in old science fiction movies. But a few things people have imagined have come true, for one, a powerful tendency toward cynicism, which, like radioactive dust after a nuclear explosion, is enveloping everything, draining it of humanity. It is a gradual shift in tone that is turning everything into pure commodity. Like a penetrating fog, its chill has filtered into hearts and minds, enveloping the entire world and freezing it, a petrifaction that enshrines impulses that were once banished to the outskirts of the soul. The distant romantic echo that had always permeated the fashion business is fading away. The larger discourse at its center, involving aesthetics, contents, adherence to reality or flight from it, is shrinking, becoming a mere exchange of data in a gigantic game of buying and selling. The impulse to shop and acquire seems to be all that remains. Cultural and social values, once so important, now seem passé, remnants of a naive, almost forgotten world. "The sector has changed radically," Armani said. "Everything changed with the arrival of Mr. Arnault [Bernard Arnault, president of LVMH], Mr. Pinault [François Pinault, president of the Pinault-Printemps-Redoute Group], and Mr. De Sole [Domenico De Sole, president of Gucci]. They are the ones who began to turn this business into something else." In response to a question concerning the importance of brand name, image, and advertising, elements that now seem to have become more important than the quality of the product, he answered decisively: "That's exactly how it is. If a brand name is 'pumped up,' heavily advertised, then customers will buy, with no regard to the product. They do it because it is fashionable. There are those who think that they're miserable peasants unless they have a Gucci wallet or a pair of Prada shoes. And an Armani jacket, I should add. These are trends. And this is one of the reasons why I feel so profoundly frustrated." This statement is significant, because the frustration it expresses is not the criticism of some small-time, aspiring fashion designer, lost in his private domain, too much of a poetic dreamer to succeed in the world of fashion, but instead an evaluation by one of the most skilled entrepreneurs in the industry. Armani doesn't like noise and commotion for its own sake: "When I started out, people hoped to make a good product and earn good money. It was a natural, physiological growth, at the foundation of which lay a worthwhile product. But it is no longer like that. Roughly speaking, it's the opposite now: nowadays the big groups decide to launch a certain name. Maybe the product is nothing special, but they make sure that this name becomes accepted even before it proves it deserves that acceptance."

The castle of Armani was built out of his own talent and a clear need: to find a personal identity and to offer aesthetic responses to a society undergoing a total transformation. He did it very well, carving out a prestigious place for himself in the world, selecting an autonomous path. The paragons whom he aspired to emulate were Chanel and Yves Saint Laurent: "They modernized fashion, bringing it in line with the way people wanted to live nowadays. They allowed people to live differently through their clothing. They didn't create apparel, they created a different society." He added: "I have tried to conceive of a new modernity, a new elegance. It isn't easy because sometimes reality moves so quickly that nobody knows what is going on, and moreover it seems that people actually want to be shocked: they are searching for explosive fashions, for things that leave them openmouthed. Instead, I try to avoid all that, because explosions don't last very long, they disappear immediately, and afterward nothing is left but the ashes." It is precisely the acceptance of the pace of his slow evolution that has taken him so far. He invented a new way of expressing elegance by triggering a great initial revolution and then introducing many small advances, all clustered around the central core of what constitutes his style.

But even if everything is moving at a different rate now, this has done nothing to undermine the substance of the Armani empire, which in the year 2000 extended around the world, with 129 Emporio Armani retail outlets and 53 Giorgio Armani boutiques. By now it covers every imaginable sector: from menswear and womenswear to childrenswear, jeans, underwear, swimsuits, and sportswear. Of course, accessories play an important role, too. But whereas for many well-known names, such as Prada, Gucci, and Louis Vuitton, shoes, bags, and leather goods play a more important role than clothing, things are different for Armani. His apparel and suits are still the main focus of production and sales, even though perfumes, eyeglasses, ties, watches, and shoes also account for a major share, rich in as-yet-unachieved potential, to such a degree that in September 1999 the company announced the creation of the Armani Accessories division. On that occasion, Armani availed himself of the authoritative expertise of Dawn Mello and Associates, a company founded by Dawn Mello herself, well known as the longtime creative director of Gucci and for having discovered Tom Ford. In 2001 the first Armani Accessories store was opened, in Milan. Many of the accessories would be produced in specialized workshops in Tuscany.

In 2002 Armani broke off his relationship with Luxottica, for fourteen years the manufacturer of Armani eyeglasses (the product line was reassigned to Sàfilo). This was no caprice but based on a substantial disagreement between Luxottica's Leonardo Del Vecchio and Armani, who did not agree with the company's methods of distribution and was also keenly interested in updating the style of the eyeglasses. The switch caused Luxottica's stock to plummet by 13.55 percent on Italy's stock market, immediately following news of the break.

Other strategic changes had already been instituted. In October 1999 another major separation was announced: a break from Armani's historic partner, GFT, now controlled by the HDP Group. Armani accused the company, which was undergoing a period of manufacturing and financial crisis, of "being characterized at this point by a total lack of direction, in the aftermath of Marco Rivetti's departure." Although he did not entirely rule out the possibility of returning to work with GFT, Giorgio was obliged to declare: "Unless the future is clear, I cannot continue here." His plan was to take away the production of the menswear lines from the Piedmont-based textiles company and produce them himself: "Even though I will move cautiously, to keep from creating problems. I already created problems by taking away the womenswear line [which he had been producing himself for a few months]. In the menswear sector, this is a fantastic company, but I have to make sure I have a certain continuity." In spring 2000 Armani made an agreement with GFT for the acquisition of the industrial cutting and assembly operations of the Giorgio Armani Collezioni and the Mani lines and also took control of distribution of the two lines in the United States. That same year, he established a joint venture with Ermenegildo Zegna, one of the most prestigious names in the high-end men's textile and apparel sector, for the production and distribution of Armani Collezioni and Mani for men; the following year, in 2001, he established another joint venture with Vestimenta. Control of the two companies remained in Armani's hands. The new corporate strategy also called for a number of other acquisitions, including the Maglificio Deanna (knitwear factory) in 2002 and the majority holding of the shoe manufacturer I Guardi. In 2001 Armani also became, through a public stock offering, the sole owner of Simint, which was consequently delisted from the Milanese Borsa. At this point, all formal apparel was produced directly by Armani himself.

In the year 2000 Giuseppe Brusone, for many years Armani's right-hand man in terms of finance and the supervisor of the company's gradual process of industrial acquisitions, left the Giorgio Armani company. His vision and Armani's had always been at odds. The possible quotation on the stock exchange and the regularly rejected offers of partnership seem to have been the ultimate cause of what the press reported as a full-fledged rift, a divorce of sorts, carried out among insinuations and hypotheses that were never confirmed.

Also in 2000, in June, another, very real source of grief welled up: Giorgio Armani's mother, Maria Raimondi, died, the female figure who had done so much to make him who he was, the woman who inspired him and in whom—as well as in his sister, Rosanna—he recognized an extraordinary moral authority. "His mother was a very important person throughout his entire life," Leo Dell'Orco tells us. "Every chance he got he would go to have dinner at her house." And Suzy Menkes recalls: "Once day, I was running over to Dolce and Gabbana, in the Via Santa Cecilia, and I happened to meet Armani. I asked him if he was designing their collection as well. He smiled and told me that his mother lived there, and that he was going to have dinner with her." Armani himself stated in an interview that he always carried a picture of her with him: "If I forget it, I send my driver to get it, I miss her if she's not with me." The void remained unhealable, and it would once again put to the test the man behind the stainless-steel, imperturbable image, the man who aroused the admiration and envy of one and all.

In September 1999 Armani presented his womenswear collection for summer 2000 in a space he had recently purchased, the former Nestlé's factory in the area around Porta Genova, in the southern part of Milan, which would soon become a new fashion mecca. The runway presentation proved to be fresh and linear. The silhouette adhered closely to the body, and an array of fasteners made the jackets, draping over the hips, particularly modern. Sarongs, bustiers, shades, and prints were based on the style of Wassily Kandinsky. The advertising campaign for that season, assigned to Ellen von Unwerth, featured surprisingly vivid colors. Immediately afterward, work began on the renovation of the 130,000-square-foot structure that would house the Armani Teatro, which Armani conceived as the new venue for seasonal appointments as well as the setting for many other initiatives, spectacles, and film showings. The historic little theater in the Via Borgonuovo 21—which had been damaged by fire in June 2001—had become too small. A much larger space was need to accommodate the growing international audience. The intimacy offered by the old address would now be reserved for the few guests invited to more exclusive and personal events.

Detractors criticized the new Teatro, designed by Tadao Ando, as excessively chilly and impersonal. But it satisfied all the functional requirements and corresponded to the purest Armani style: "I like the concept of eternity expressed in this work," he commented on the day of the inauguration. "It is something that endures, it is not tied to the instant, and it offers a substance that will allow it to continue to be valid for many years to come, in this somewhat sterile setting." The structure is both spare and monumental, with large fixed backdrops that alternate with light structures to produce slashes of illumination, breaking up the expanse of gray cement. A long corridor leading to the theater, which is built according to the principle of flexibility and variegated use, creates interesting interplays of perception and architectural elevations. A line of slender columns with a square section detached from the ceiling creates a series of bewildering optical adventures, the gaze finally reconciled by the view of the small internal lake. Everything is disciplined yet crude, austere, waiting for a human presence to enliven it. "My clothing, in order to be represented at its best, requires large, clean, modern rooms," Armani explained. He is especially sensitive to the relationship between space and fashion. "It isn't true that a collection can be presented anywhere. In order to fully understand my style you need a special setting designed expressly for it." And Tadao Ando declared: "I am interested in the fact that architecture can give people energy, especially in places where they gather, so that when this space houses runway presentations, and many people will come together here, there will be a powerful exchange, an intense communication, and it will be possible to feel how this place amplifies the energy of those who gather here." The official inauguration took place in 2001.

Armani's presence in the city became all the more noticeable with the opening, in 2000, of a major store on the Via Manzoni. The space, which for years had contained one of the traditional cafés of the upper middle classes in Milan, the Alemagna, was now a spectacular showcase for Giorgio Armani. He had purchased it in 1998, for 125 billion lire, from the Italian insurance conglomerate Assicurazioni Generali. Armani/Manzoni 31—this is the official name of the place—is a large commercial space devoted to a single label: when you enter it, you are totally immersed in Armani. The megastore represents him nicely: it seems discreet and understated, but in reality it is imposing and authoritative. It contains a little of everything: on the three floors, linked by a wide escalator, you can find not only a large Sony corner shop but also an Emporio Armani, an Armani Jeans corner shop, an Armani perfume shop, Armani flowers, Armani books, a very popular café, a Nobu Japanese restaurant, and, naturally, the newborn Armani Casa. In 2002 an Armani Dolci (a sweetshop) was added to the selection, followed in 2003 by Armani Privé, a very exclusive lounge bar where almost every evening, at the traditional Italian hour of the aperitif, you can run into Giorgio Armani himself.

To his already substantial array of dwellings he added an apartment in Paris, upstairs from the Saint Germain Emporio Armani. It comprised 2,150 square feet, furnished with the finds from a single day's frantic foraging through the Porte de Vanves street fair, where, as he himself admits, he enjoys haggling over prices, even though in those years he was officially the largest taxpayer in all Italy (his comment: "I am not the richest one, I am just the most honest one").

The new Casa line was officially presented in September 2000, but it had been part of Armani's plans for a long time. It was in the nature of things that he should wind up producing it: "For three reasons: the first was that it was a logical business. We wanted to differentiate the company in a new direction, other than ready-to-wear. The second reason is that it was a way of putting my ego in the forefront, of proving to myself that I can succeed in different sectors of fashion." The third reason was that it gave Armani a chance to offer furniture that he wanted to see in his own homes. As time passed and his real estate holdings increased, his expertise in furnishing grew apace, to the point that he declared: "I once had a blind respect for interior decorators, probably because I had no experience, and I didn't know any better than to entrust the job to specialists. Then I realized, to an increasing degree, that my ideas were every bit as good as theirs. Architects and interior decorators are often too indulgent with themselves, they are more interested in designing for themselves and for their competitors, but they do it at your expense." After a few not very satisfactory experiments, Armani came to the conclusion that a home must respect its owner's notion of intimacy and should not be furnished in order to "comply with the tastes of some glossy magazine." He set out to design extremely concrete furniture, following a modular concept that would allow a personal interpretation of style.

Some critics obsessed with modernism and a different idea of fashion accused Armani of being popular with the least interesting sector of the establishment. Giorgio allowed these challenges to slide off him, aware that his approach was a winner, regardless of any jibes that fashion victims might hurl. Maintaining one's equilibrium with such integrity will always attract opposition: "When I created trousers with volants, Suzy Menkes said: 'When will Armani go back to making suits?' But when I make suits, I become dull and old-fashioned, and people say that there is no innovation and that I am not part of any particular trend." According to Patrick McCarthy, those who are interested in trendy fashion should look to someone else: "If that is the kind of fashion you are looking for, Armani is not the right man for you. And he shouldn't be. When he tries to be, I believe that he makes a mistake. There are times when he gives in to the pressure that I believe comes mainly from the press. Because the press can represent a negative factor for fashion designers, who feel a need to appear on the cover of *WWD*, *W*, or *Vogue* or who must convince young movie stars to wear their clothing and therefore feel a need to be trendy." Trendy or no, the fact remains that, according to a survey carried out in 2005 in the United States, the Luxury Brand Status Research and 2005 Luxury Status Index, issued by the Luxury Institute, the name Armani is one of the most attractive status symbols around. Among fashion labels, he is trailed by Hermès and Prada.

In 2000 Armani Cosmetics was founded, a new perfume, Mania, was also presented, and the long list of awards and recognitions assigned to the fashion designer continued to grow, among them, the David di Donatello—the Italian Oscar—for his contributions to cinema, presented to him by his friend Lauren Hutton. But the most significant celebration of his achievements was held at the Solomon R. Guggenheim Museum in New York: a major exhibition, curated by Germano Celant and Harold Koda. "Giorgio Armani: A Retrospective" displayed more than five hundred suits that furnished an overview of the designer's three-decade-long career. The doors of the famous museum, traditionally devoted to modern art, opened up for the first time to a celebration of a fashion designer.

People gossiped about the generous donation Armani had made to the Guggenheim—the figure of $15 million came up frequently—speculating on its role in the decision of the director, Tom Krens, to launch the exhibition. Debate was raging over the real purpose of cultural institutions and their sudden alliance with major trademarks and labels. The Armani show was by no means the first: The Metropolitan Museum had already hosted a show on Cartier jewelry, and the Museum of Modern Art had devoted an exhibition to Ferrari. Two years before the Armani retrospective, the Guggenheim had hosted a show on motorcycles, sponsored by BMW. But the Armani show was a major media event: "Frank Lloyd Wright, the Guggenheim's architect, would have loved this show. Wright cared a lot about clothes," wrote Herbert Muschamp in the *New York Times*, going so far as to identify a powerful analogy between the museum's spiral structure and the fashion on exhibit: "They are both signs of life." Praise was lavished on Robert Wilson's installation, which created the impression of being inside one of Noguchi's paper lanterns; there was more than one description of the collage of religious and exotic sounds constructed by Michael Galasso as an aural accompaniment to the visual display; and exalted tones were used to honor the talent and eclecticism of this fashion designer who had been so often the victim of dismissive preconception. Known primarily for having put "power suits" on women and men, for his use of greige, for a range of color shades ranging from sand to mud, it was now widely discovered that Armani was much more than that. "I like Giorgio for his men's and women's suits," Patrick McCarthy tells us, "but he has a twofold mind: on the one hand, he is very rigorous, and on the other, he is very imaginative. I also like his evening gowns:

some of them are just magnificent. When he lets himself go, he will always surprise you: you never expect this celebration of the female figure by someone who designs suits."

The exhibition was mounted in various cities around the world over the course of the years that followed, in the Bilbao Guggenheim, in the Berlin Neue Nationalgalerie, and in the spaces of the Royal Academy of Arts in Burlington Gardens, London. In Italy, the show was installed in the magnificent setting of the Baths of Diocletian, in Rome. Then came stops in Tokyo, Los Angeles, and, in 2006, Shanghai. Armani's plan calls for the final, definitive exhibition in this world tour to be in a new space, which should be ready by 2008, near the Armani Teatro, in Milan, where all the material exhibited will find a permanent home.

On September 11, 2001, Giorgio Armani was in New York, in SoHo, preparing the opening of the new Armani Casa boutique, when one of his coworkers called him and told him to turn on the television. At that exact moment the second airplane was crashing into one of the Twin Towers. "The whole world was horrified in the face of this catastrophe. Later, I made sure that all my coworkers returned safely to Milan. The shop was opened, but in an empty neighborhood close to the ruins, which sent up a steady stream of smoke. For the moment, there was practically no one around, of course, but I still hope that the people of New York want to forget about the tragedy and go on with their lives. Having said that, it was a genuine blow in financial terms." I still remember meeting Roberta Armani in Milan during the runway presentations for spring-summer 2002, which came shortly after the attacks in New York. She always traveled with her uncle on business, and she told me with great emotion about her personal experience of the tragedy, the fear she had felt, and the difficulties and anxiety involved in finding a plane to get back home.

The tragic events of September 11, aside from their emotional impact and the ramifications on the political stage, also had a major effect on the economy. Just two months later, Armani spoke of a 20 percent decline in sales in the United States. "The biggest effect came about in the area around New York City; less on the West Coast," he said. "Europe remained stable, with a strengthening of the market in Italy, in the United Kingdom, and in France. The Japanese market remained solid, while South Korea grew. We are in any case happy to announce that we expect to reach the 2001 target for at least a 20 percent increase in revenue." The financial solidity of the Giorgio Armani company allowed it to continue to open new retail space, as in Moscow in November 2001, at number 1 on the Tretyakovsky Proezd Street, and to land at number 2 on one of the best-known streets on earth: Via Montenapoleone, in Milan.

There is no question that September 11 was a watershed, to the point of substantially modifying society's attitude to consumption. "I don't think that things will ever go back quite to the way they were," Armani said. "It will take a long time before people have the same enthusiasm." One of the reasons his company has suffered less than others has to do with the fact that the business is not focused on accessories, which form part of the standard offerings in airport duty-free shops. Instead, Armani is strong in suits, which have another type of distribution network. Once again, time has proven Armani right: his prudent business management, which kept him from accepting offers to be absorbed by larger groups or making reckless acquisitions, was farsighted. If you ask him what his greatest quality is, he will say, "I believe in my ideas. If I happen not to follow my instincts, then it's almost certain that I will make a wrong decision. That's how it always goes. I know when I am right, and that is my greatest strength."

The prestigious Pirelli calendar for 2002 was shot by Peter Lindbergh, making use exclusively of Armani outfits, and that same year the documentary *My Voyage to Italy*, directed by Martin Scorsese, was presented to the press. The movie lasted four hours and was seven years in preparation. Scorsese had the idea in 1995, when his friend Giorgio came to visit him on the set of *Casino*, in Las Vegas. Armani immediately warmed to the project and invested $250,000 to become the executive producer. "We have often talked with a great shared love for Italian cinema," Martin Scorsese declared, "and I knew how Giorgio loved it. And so, for me, it was a natural thing to get him involved." The director gives Armani credit for having kept the project alive during the first two years. "I could see how much Giorgio loved Visconti, and he wanted to be sure that we accorded sufficient space in the movie to *Ossessione*, which Giorgio called 'the Bible.' And when I showed him the card-playing sequence in De Sica's *L'oro di Napoli* [*The Gold of Naples*], he asked me to keep every last frame." Armani liked the idea of tying his name to Scorsese's film: "For the future, for posterity," he said at one point. "Like Scorsese, I want to keep alive the history of cinema and give something back to Italian cinema, since I have worked with so many American movie productions. I also wanted this movie to be a testament for the future generations of Italian directors." During the course of production, another initiative developed as well, which led to a collaboration with the Mediaset television group. *Cinema Forever* was meant to bring about the restoration of a number of historical Italian movies, some of which would be shown at the Armani Teatro.

Also in 2002 he launched the perfume Sensi; the advertising campaign was assigned to Zhang Yimou, director of *Raise the Red Lantern*. The choice once again demonstrated Armani's keen intuition and was further proof that he was ahead of the curve in terms of image in communications. The ad campaign coincided with a radical increase in contacts with the East, including the opening of an Armani Collezioni shop in Kiev, right next to the cathedral of Saint Sophia, in partnership with the well-known Ukrainian soccer player Andriy Shevchenko. During the same period, a new Armani Casa space was opened in Beijing, and the boutique, which dated back to 1998, received a new facade: "The store had been designed according to a somewhat romantic idea of the Far East. I personally wanted a big red portal. That was a mistake. The Chinese love European style, and that's what they want to see in their own country, exactly as it was in Europe." Armani has always been fascinated with the exotic: "In my collections, there has always been a clearly identifiable Eastern element. But," he admits, "my salespeople in Japan, for instance, told me that Japanese women prefer to dress in Occidental style." He will now have a presence in Shenzhen as well, with an Armani Collezioni shop, and will inaugurate a megastore in Hong Kong that will bring together all the labels in the Armani Group. The Armani Charter House extends over thirty-two thousand square feet on three floors in the Central District. The architects Claudio Silvestrin and Massimiliano Fuksas worked on the project, inventing a chromatic itinerary that accompanies the visitors along a spiral path. The building features a light, transparent structure, in curved glass and steel. In Shanghai, the ground floor of a thirties-era skyscraper now houses a Giorgio Armani and Armani Casa sales outlet.

The development of the Chinese market was unstoppable. Armani was hailed as a star there, and in 2004 he organized two runway presentations, one in Shanghai, where another major shop was inaugurated in the heart of the fashionable Bund district, and one in a second shop in Hong Kong. The tour was transformed into a veritable victory lap. All the events were televised, and the viewing audience was gigantic. Armani returned to China in 2006, for the inauguration of his traveling exhibition, which opened in Shanghai. The Chinese market is exceedingly attractive, with nearly a hundred million newly wealthy potential consumers who look to the West with an enthusiasm comparable to the West's recurring obsession with a mythic Orient (the exotic is a relative concept). The Far East in particular has a powerful fascination with Italian fashion labels, corresponding to the beginning of the cultural curve that Western nations have already completed. This immense opportunity is the flip side of the problems the Italian textile industry is experiencing as it daily battles against the relentless competition of the Chinese textile industry.

Even though Giorgio Armani doesn't particularly like to fly, he travels around the world as casually as you might go to the countryside for the weekend, and with an enviable level of energy. He is driven by an unappeasable curiosity, and, now more than ever before, he expresses the wish to be loved by the younger generations. It was precisely to establish his familiarity with the world of youth that in 2004 he began sponsoring a Milanese basketball team, Olimpia—once the historic Simmenthal—that was experiencing financial difficulties (it is now called the Armani Jeans team). This move reflected specific marketing instincts, but it was also a sentimental gesture, an homage to his late brother, Sergio, who had played basketball when he was a young man.

Armani looks at the changing world with unflagging interest; the passing years seem to do nothing to undermine his focus on new design. He has won it all. He is wealthier than any of his colleagues. But in July 2004 he chose to celebrate his seventieth birthday at the Locanda del Falco, in Rivalta, near Piacenza, with thirty-five carefully chosen guests: only relatives, friends, and his closest coworkers. When someone asked him where the Hollywood stars were, Giorgio Armani answered: "A birthday is a meaningful, private event; you should only celebrate with truly important people. This, in particular, is a truly special birthday because I am crossing the threshold of my seventieth year. That is why I chose to have with me those who are closest to me in my life and my work." He also took this opportunity to tell an editor of *La Libertà*, the local daily newspaper: "Here in Rivalta, as in Piacenza, I feel at home, which is why I have said, and I repeat, that I wouldn't mind living out my old age here." It is in Rivalta that the bodies of his brother and his mother are laid to rest, upon whose graves—which Armani visits every chance he gets—a bunch of fresh flowers is laid every day. Flowing nearby is the river that was the setting for so many long-ago moments of happiness: "For me, the river Trebbia," says Armani, "has always been synonymous with holidays, ever since I was a child and we used to go swimming there. Often, there was no water at all, but even just walking on the rocky riverbed gave us the feeling that we were, so to speak, in an exotic setting."

Talk of retirement notwithstanding, not a year since Armani was awarded the first plaque in the new Walk of Style in Los Angeles, on Rodeo Drive, which is the counterpart for the fashion world of the movies' Walk of Fame. And the most recent birthday present Armani gave himself was a 160-foot sailboat, built by the Codecasa Shipyards in Viareggio; he christened the boat *Mariù*, another homage to his mother. "It took twenty years for me to make this decision," he admits. "After the death of Sergio [Galeotti] I started renting a sailboat. Then I thought to myself, why shouldn't I buy myself one, if I wanted? I have enough money. This is truly the one luxury I've decided to indulge in." In perfect Armani style, the interior of the boat is decorated in a functional and geometric style. The floor is constructed of elegant teak boards, the same kind of wood that is usually used as exterior decking; titanium slabs cover the ceiling, and the windows are large and panoramic. An elevator connects three floors of commodious living space: six cabins with six bathrooms, enough to accommodate up to twelve guests, tended by a crew of twelve, all dressed in Emporio Armani. His collection of homes has grown as well. In 2002 he added a wing to the castle of San Giorgio, in Portofino, next door to Rosanna's house. The following year, during a vacation in Antigua, he fell in love with a beachfront villa that was for sale. Of course, he bought it. "When he is at Broni he wishes he could be on Pantelleria. If he is at Pantelleria he wants to be in Saint-Tropez, and when he is at Saint-Tropez, he wishes he could go to Forte dei Marmi," Leo Dell'Orco says with amusement. "He likes houses. He likes to build them, he likes to watch them take form. He is unlikely to buy a house and leave it as it was. The house on Antigua, for instance, where you can step right down onto the beach, would have been perfect exactly as it was. But he had to change it completely. He put in his own furniture, he made it the way he wanted it." Testimony to his aesthetic restlessness and his unquenchable lust for life, just three years after the launch of the *Mariù*, he is already planning a larger boat. "Not a sailboat," Dell'Orco point out, "because that requires too much time. A motorboat is faster."

Armani's whole life has been a breathless race, chasing after goals that shift a little further into the distance each time he thinks he has attained them. Now, at last, he has the pleasure of allowing himself a little leisure and enjoyment, a little fun, to do what he wants to do, without worrying that he will no longer live up to the clichés everyone knows. This new phase in his life has also led to a visible change in his fashion. For the past few seasons, Armani has introduced elements that dismay those who are nostalgic for his old rigor. His womenswear is now much softer. He has gone so far as to include slits, jabots, draperies, and the entire apparatus of seduction that until just recently he had rejected entirely. This is clear in his collection for winter 2006–2007: he has rounded off the cuts and amused himself by playing with all the signifiers of femininity. The skirts are clingy and draped, or, if they have a straight fall, they end with a small flounce. Paired with high heels, small hats, and tiny purses, they re-create a calm, cadenced step and posture from days gone by. The jackets are constructed and short, embellished with a bow in the back and lapels of an unusual size. The colors are creamy, grenadine, amethyst, midnight blue. It is a fashion that seems like an expression of the desire for a lifestyle reserved for a very few, that takes you far away from reality. Armani does not like to be a prisoner of his own image. Now he feels a new freedom, a freedom to contradict himself and even to displease those who expect something else from him. Ignoring all the polemics that raged after that provocative statement of his in 2002—"By now, even the word *luxury* is disgusting"—Armani surprised everyone with a high-fashion line, which he presented in January 2005 in Paris.

"The Privé collection is a concession that he can certainly afford," Patrick McCarthy tells us, "because Armani is wealthier than anyone else, but he also represents an idea of smart business. And Giorgio has a flexible mind, which always seeks out good business. There is no real reason for him to do haute-couture runway presentations in Paris: he indulged in this just to show that he could do it. He wanted to try it out, and then, once he had done it, he realized that it offered something special to his public. There is already Chanel, Saint Laurent, I might say Lagerfeld, and there is Signor Armani. These are the four major figures in the fashion of our time." Privé is simply a statement, a way he has of amusing himself, taking on the challenge of working on different terrain. He debuted in a spare, unadorned space in the Rue Lauriston, quite different from what one might have expected: "This loft represents modernity," Armani explained. "I wanted to do something new, the atelier with stuccoes is obsolete by now, it would have interfered with the rigor of my simple clothing, my black and white. My coworkers were perplexed, they wanted me to take into account the sort of coquetries to which the clients of haute couture are accustomed. But I wanted to change register." He amazed the few guests attending by displaying evening gowns with sinuous and clinging silhouettes. The chest was still taut, constructed, while the flowing skirt terminated in a profusion of fabric, a liquid godet. There were embroideries, jewels, and the inevitable little hats. The source of inspiration was the elegance of the early twentieth century. "This was a form of experimentation," Armani commented. The third Privé collection, Mirroir, presented on January 23, 2006, on the catwalks of Parisian haute couture, won general acclaim. He staged a spectacle of lightness, interplays of volumes, and shades of color that even included sophisticated dark blue costume jewelry and crystals for jackets, and suits with ample, flowing lines, all definitely worthy of Armani's finest presentations at their most exclusive.

This is the luxury he allowed himself: the luxury of doing what he likes. Armani has made incursions into every world imaginable: aside from his tireless collaboration with the world of the cinema, with the theater, and with music, in 2003 he also designed uniforms for the English national soccer team, and in 2006 he played a major role in the Turin Olympics: after joining the procession following the torchbearer through the streets of Milan, he helped make the inaugural ceremonies more enjoyable by designing the clothing for Carla Bruni, who carried the Italian flag into the Olympic Stadium dressed in a long white outfit. In 2005 he even oversaw the design of a limited series of convertible coupes for Mercedes Benz, designing the color scheme and the interiors of the Giorgio Armani CLK 500. Tireless and increasingly an entrepreneur and businessman, in 2004 he signed a letter of intent for the creation of a string of luxury hotels with a Dubai company, Emaar Properties. His role would be to supply the furniture—Armani Casa, of course—for all the hotels, which would be built in the years to come in various cities around the world. The first hotels to be finished would be in Dubai and Milan (2008). Yet even with all this, fashion remained in first place: in June 2006 the creation of the menswear line Giorgio Armani fatto a Mano su Misura [Made to Measure] was announced.

Armani also engaged with worldwide issues. In January 2006 he spoke at Davos, at the World Economic Forum, announcing his support for RED, an economic initiative launched by Bono and Bobby Shriver in support of the Global Fund, with contributions by American Express, Converse, and The Gap. He also designed a specific line of products the proceeds from the sale of which would be earmarked for the fight against AIDS, tuberculosis, and malaria in Africa.

The Gruppo Armani is now one of the largest manufacturing groups in the world of fashion, with forty-nine hundred employees and thirteen plants. The company's solidity is confirmed by its consolidated net revenue in 2005: 1.428 billion euros, an increase of 10 percent. It has achieved many goals recently, principal among them the success—in critical and economic terms—of the haute couture collection and a new joint venture with Como Holdings for the expansion of the A/X Armani Exchange label.

The possibility of being quoted on the stock exchange was announced in an interview published on April 10, 2006, in the *Wall Street Journal*. When asked about the future of the company, of which he is sole shareholder, president, and managing director, Giorgio Armani stated: "The most reasonable solution may well be the stock market, even though that would practically change nothing as far as I am concerned, because I want to stay here to do my work, make my decisions." He also stated that many different hypotheses are conceivable, though he ruled out the possibility of acquisition by a financial institution, "because we definitely don't need money." And he went on: "Five years ago, I said no to the stock market, but now I'm almost seventy-two years old, and I need to send a signal to the market that, even though I am a spry little old man, I have the future of the company very much at heart. I also need to send a signal to the people who work here. That doesn't mean that we have started to think of an IPO [initial public offering].

We haven't set up a team to work on this yet, nor have we appointed an investment bank to help us." Concerning the eternal question of a possible creative director for his company, he said: "There are two or three people who are very close to me, upon whom I can rely, and they are my two nieces [Silvana and Roberta] and my nephew [Andrea Camerana]. For the menswear sector, there is a person who has been with me for many years [Leo Dell'Orco] who could be the director of the menswear line. Of course, I will need to try things out. Now, these people have my protection: if there are doubts, they can come to me. One day in the future, it will be their turn to make the decisions." No hypothesis, then, of a creative director from some other fashion house: "In any case," Armani points out with great firmness, "anyone who has come to work here from the outside has rapidly become an 'Armanian,' losing any frivolous and experimental identity. Here, we don't do experimental collections. We have collections that sell and collections that don't sell."

And so everything is wide open, because stepping away from all that he has created would be an unthinkable sacrifice for Giorgio Armani. The company is his great achievement—he himself has compared it to a son—and the everyday commitment to making it grow and succeed is a tyrannical, absolute presence in his life, in the shadow of which he has taken shelter, protecting himself from the tempests of emotion. Like a solitary samurai, he has led a life of self-denial and discipline. This clean, austere, Calvinistic man is even harder on himself than on others. What he fears most in life is disease and the loss of the people whom he loves: "And that is why I am always afraid, someday in the future, of finding myself in the position of an elderly, wealthy gentleman surrounded by people who are with me only because I am wealthy, people who spend time with me, not for myself, but for my money."

Armani claims to have a very simple, direct, and straightforward mind-set. He is obsessed by the need to maintain control of himself and everything around him; he is respected but also greatly feared. He also has a lighter, more playful nature, which he reveals to only a few people. It is interesting to note the dichotomy between his entrepreneurial courage, that warriorlike approach to his work, and his fear of exposing himself personally, his reluctance to open up, his fear of being hurt. This vulnerability may be the most fascinating aspect of his personality, all the more so now that he has built his empire. Even now, he is not satisfied: "Of course, none of us ever stops learning how to live. But it would take me another lifetime to take advantage of the money that I have earned. I have invested years of hard work, the most important years in a man's life. And even though I am happy with what I have achieved and what I have done, sometimes it seems to me that everything happened so quickly, perhaps all too fast, in too much of a hurry."

Bibliography

Blonsky, Marshall. *American Mythologies.* New York: Oxford University Press, 1992.

Bocca, Giorgio. *Metropolis.* Milan: Mondadori, 1993.

Butazzi, Grazietta, and Alessandra Mottola Molfino. *La moda italiana. Dall'antimoda allo stilismo.* Milan: Electa, 1987.

Carter, Ernestine. *The Changing World of Fashion.* New York: G. P. Putnam, 1977.

Dictionnaire de la mode au XXe siècle. Paris: Editions du Regard, 1994.

Ginsborg, Paul. *Storia d'Italia dal dopoguerra ad oggi.* Turin: Einaudi, 1989.

Giorgio Armani. New York: Guggenheim Museum, 2000.

Harrison, Martin. *Appearances. Fashion Photography Since 1945.* London: Jonathan Cape, 1991.

Lurie, Alison. *The Language of Clothes.* London: Bloomsbury, 1981.

Mereghetti, Paolo (ed.). *Dizionario dei film.* Milan: Baldini Castoldi Dalai *editore,* 2000.

Molho, Renata. "Il futuro è già passato." In *Gli anni '60. Le immagini al potere.* Milan: Mazzotta, 1996.

La Storia. Turin: UTET, 2004.

Vergani, Guido (ed.). *Dizionario della moda.* Milan: Baldini Castoldi Dalai *editore,* 2004.

Articles and Interviews

FROM: *Abitare, Amica, Bunte, Chicago Tribune, China Daily, Il Corriere della Sera, Corriere Magazine, D di Repubblica, DNR, Domus, The Economist, Elle France, Elle Italia, Epoca, L'Espresso, Esquire, L'Europeo, Le Figaro, The Financial Times, Forbes, Gente, Il Giornale, Il Giornale di Sicilia, Il Giorno, GQ, GQ Japan, Grazia, The Guardian, Harper's Bazaar, I.D., The Independent, The International Herald Tribune, Io Donna, Journal du Textile, Liberation, La Libertà, Los Angeles Times, Madame Figaro, Marie Claire, Marie Claire Italia, Marie Claire UK, Il Messaggero, MFF, Il Mondo, Mondo Economico, Movie Line, La Nazione, Newsweek, The New Yorker, The New York Times, Le Nouvel Observateur, Panorama, People, Prima Comunicazione, La Repubblica, Il Secolo XIX, Sette, Il Sole 24 Ore, La Stampa, The Sunday Telegraph, The Sunday Times, Talk USA, Time, L'Unità, L'Uomo Vogue, Vanity Fair, Il Venerdì, Ventiquattro, Vogue America, Vogue France, Vogue Homme, Vogue Italia, W, The Wall Street Journal, WWD, Yacht Capital.*